A Long Hard Road

Dreams. Detours. What Matters.

Tom Sykes

First Edition
Published by:
Otter Creek Digital Studios, Inc.
www.tomsykesmusic.com

Virginia Beach, Virginia
Cover design: Tom Sykes
Printed in the United States of America

979-8-234-04697-0

Dedication

This book is dedicated to my wife, Jamie, and my two children, Katie and Birdie, who have patiently endured years of hearing me work on music through the air vents at all hours—especially in the middle of the night, when inspiration strikes and volume control apparently becomes optional. Their love, support, and remarkable ability to sleep through repeated chorus rewrites made this book—and probably my sanity—possible.

I would also like to thank Bob and Nancy Sykes for their unwavering support.

Prologue

Born to Change the World,
Ended Up Buying it on Credit

I was born in the early Fifties, which means I grew up trying to change the world and eventually watched my generation buy it on credit.

That officially makes me a Baby Boomer. I don't remember being asked about this, but apparently it's permanent—like a tattoo you don't recall getting but everyone insists you chose.

We were the generation that was going to change everything. Idealists. Rebels. Truth seekers. Revolutionaries. Or at least that's what we told ourselves while standing around listening to records and nodding like we understood what Dylan was talking about. Half the time we didn't, but the music told us we should, and that was close enough.

We wanted to make a difference. We were against materialism and believed it was corrupting the country. Stuff was bad. Owning things meant you had sold out. To prove this, we wore blue jeans, T-shirts, and sneakers—not because they were fashionable, but because they were cheap and didn't mean anything.

Or so we said.

The truth is, we cared deeply about how those jeans fit.

And how faded they were. And whether they looked like you'd been worn in by a meaningful life. Music taught us that, too. Every album cover came with instructions—what to wear, what to think, and who you were allowed to be.

We grew our hair long to show we didn't conform to social stereotypes, which was ironic considering how much effort we put into conforming to that exact look. You couldn't just grow your hair—you had to grow it correctly. Music magazines, album jackets, and liner notes made sure you knew the difference.

We questioned everything. Government. Society. Authority. The status quo. And especially the war in Vietnam. Nothing was off-limits. If there was a rule, we wanted to know who made it, why they made it, and whether there was a song explaining how to break it.

Music wasn't background noise—it was our operating system. You didn't ask someone what they believed; you looked at their record collection. That stack of vinyl told you their politics, their attitude, and how seriously they took themselves. It also told you whether you were going to get along.

I even had a rule.

If someone owned a Carpenters album—or a Bee Gees record—or, God help them, Bread—I would run. Not walk. Run. It wasn't that they were bad people or I hated the artist. It just meant our conversations were eventually going to end in disappointment. They were a little too Pollyanna for me, and I didn't have the patience to fake enthusiasm. To us, music wasn't entertainment. It was proof. Proof you were paying attention. Proof you weren't asleep. Proof you were on the right side of things—whatever that meant at the time.

What still amazes me is how this same generation—the one that hated materialism, distrusted corporations, and thought advertising was brainwashing—eventually figured out how to sell bottled water to each other. Not just sell it, but argue about which brand tasted better.

Water.

Something we all used to drink straight out of a hose while a transistor radio played somewhere nearby.

Somewhere along the way, the music faded into the background. The soundtrack stayed, but the message got quieter. We may go down in history as the greediest and most self-centered generation ever recorded. We traded ideals for comfort, rebellion for convenience, and vinyl for whatever was easiest to play in the car.

We didn't just become what we started out hating. We became professionals at it. Put it on repeat. Turned it into a lifestyle.

For me, though, music never stayed in the background. Even before I understood what it was doing to me, it was already there—shaping how I thought, how I questioned things, and how I tried to make sense of the world. I just didn't know yet that it was going to be the one thing I never outgrew.

Anyway ... that's the backdrop.

On to my childhood.

Chapter 1

Built from Barracks, Chickens, and Bad Ideas

We lived in what was then Princess Anne County on three acres of land shared with my great-grandparents and grandparents on my mother's side. It was less a neighborhood and more a family compound—minus the uniforms, rules, and any official paperwork acknowledging how strange it probably looked from the outside.

My great-grandfather had originally built a two-story house for himself. He had to borrow money to build it. And like most things involving borrowed money, he immediately regretted it. He didn't like debt, didn't trust it, and clearly didn't want it sleeping under his roof. So he solved the problem by selling the house to my parents.

Problem solved.

They then moved into a small cottage behind the house that he had originally built as a beauty shop for my great-grandmother. She moved the beauty shop to another location, so the building was converted into their new home, which I assume worked just fine once you stopped expecting it to smell like permanent-wave solution and broken dreams.

There were four cottages on the property in total, all built by my grandfather and great-grandfather out of old military barracks. During World War II, the Navy had built extra barracks to house sailors flooding in from all over the country. When the war ended, the Navy decided they no longer needed them and offered them to locals for free—which is exactly what you want to hear when someone explains what your house is made of. The barracks were dismantled piece by piece and turned into small cottages. My grandparents lived in one while they built their dream home, which took long enough that the "temporary" cottage started to feel like a long-term commitment.

At the time, Princess Anne County was still rural and quiet—nothing like the city of Virginia Beach it would eventually become. In front of our house ran Virginia Beach Boulevard, the main road connecting Norfolk to the ocean. It was busy enough to remind you civilization existed, but not close enough to make you feel like you lived in the city. Behind our house were woods. After that came Mennonite farms and dairy farms stretching toward Kempsville. Cows were a normal part of the landscape, which kept expectations realistic.

Kempsville was originally known as Kemps Landing and had once been the county seat of Princess Anne

County. It was also where John Askew—considered the first Virginian killed in the Revolutionary War—was shot by Lord Dunmore.

So I grew up in a place made of recycled war materials, surrounded by family, farmland, and history. That's where I lived—before memory had a beginning and stories learned how to line up properly.

FAMILY

My father worked for the Norfolk Fire Department and, on his days off, did part-time work as an elevator mechanic with my grandfather on my mother's side. My mother stayed home with us. I had two older brothers—Bobby, the oldest, and Jim—who had already bonded by the time I came along, and they were inseparable. That made me the odd man out from the start.

Because of that, I spent a lot of time with my great-grandfather, and we were close. Our birthdays were only one day apart, so we celebrated together every year. People said that when he was younger, he'd been a hard-working, gruff man with a quick temper. I never saw that version. To me, he was gentle and kind, always walking around making a half-whistle, half-hissing sound under his breath. It must have been fashionable at some point, because all my grand-fathers did it.

I was lucky enough to have two sets of great-grand-parents.

My grandfather and great-grandfather on my mother's side raised a few thousand chickens on the property. They'd worked out a deal with the local feed store: we supplied the land, the store supplied the feed and chickens, and they split the profits.

One of my earliest memories is sitting in the chicken house with my great-grandfather sanding eggs.

Yes—sanding eggs.

We sanded the dirt and chicken poop off them so they'd look presentable before being sold. Apparently, even eggs had standards. The chicken house was a long building divided into sections by chicken wire, with roosts in every section. There was a wooden trolley so feed bags could be moved from room to room. I'd sit on top of those bags and ride along while he fed the chickens, which felt perfectly normal at the time. My poor man's Disneyland.

I also learned very early that being barefoot around chickens was a terrible idea. I'm honestly amazed I didn't die of some mysterious chicken-related disease that would later be named after me.

I didn't have long with him. He died when I was very young. I remember the day clearly. My mother was checking something baking in the oven when my great-grandmother yelled for her from the front door of her cottage about thirty feet away. My mother let the oven door fall open and ran outside. I remember the sound of her voice and knowing instantly that something was very wrong. The ambulance came quickly—the fire station was just down the street. I ran upstairs and watched from the window as they rushed in and out, then carried him out completely covered with a sheet. That was my first real experience with mortality. I didn't understand it. I just knew I missed him deeply.

Family was everywhere. Cousins on both sides, all close in age. We didn't have much money, so entertainment was something we invented ourselves. We built tree forts, dug underground tunnels, and roamed the woods until dark.

Looking back, that life kept me grounded. It felt like something straight out of *The Andy Griffith Show*.

We had very few neighbors. The ones we had raised sheep or horses and kept large gardens.

One of my favorite places was the feed store. Old men sat in a circle of chairs in the back, telling stories about earlier times and handing out advice whether you asked for it or not. The floors were worn wooden planks, everything coated in dust, and feed bags were stacked everywhere. To this day, whenever I see a red-and-white checkerboard pattern, I think of chickens' poop between my toes.

As a child, I often felt left out, though I didn't always know what I was left out of. I never liked the herd mentality. I wanted to go my own way.

I spent hours in my imagination. "What if?" and "Why?" were the games I played most. What if I could fly? Walk through walls? Why did Superman wear long johns with his underwear on the outside? Why do we say war is bad but teach how it solved America's problems?

Being the youngest meant hand-me-down clothes. Iron-on patches must have been popular, because every pair of jeans I owned had one peeling off—usually on the knees. My brothers' patches were always on the butt, which led me to believe their farts were powerful enough to blow holes straight through denim.

We made our own toys. A 2×4 and a piece of water pipe could become a gun. Dirt-clod fights were serious business. Wet mud packed into a pipe could be launched at terrifying speed. I ended up in the hospital once after one of those hit me in the eye.

Looking back, pipes were disturbingly versatile weapons.

We weren't allowed to cross Virginia Beach Boulevard —it was too busy. Unfortunately, there was a Coke machine outside the little store on the other side, and to us that might as well have been a religious experience. So we found another way. A drainage pipe ran under the road and emptied into a ditch in our yard. When it dried out, we crawled through it. Bobby went first with a flashlight. I followed. Jim brought up the rear. Halfway through, Bobby screamed—there was a rat. Bobby started backing up. Jim tried to turn around and got stuck. Bobby backed into me, I kicked Jim, and all I could picture was a rat charging toward us with dinner plans.

We never made it to that Coke machine.

Being indoors was never an option, so we kept building stuff outdoors. My grandfather brought us lumber from elevator equipment crates, and we used it for tree forts and underground tunnels—holes with wooden roofs covered in dirt and weeds. They usually lasted until the first big rain.

One year, Pop—our name for my grandfather—drove a massive tiller straight into one of our forgotten tunnels. Pop had a legendary temper. Getting that tiller out was not a pleasant experience. When Pop got mad, underground suddenly felt like a very sensible place to be.

Another year, my brother Jim decided to create an amusement park. I was the test pilot. The first ride was a wash bucket tied to a rope between two trees. I slid about two feet and got dumped on the ground like a sack of potatoes. The second ride was a cable stretched from a tree to the chicken house with a pulley handle. I couldn't touch the ground, so I slammed into the chicken house at full speed, burst through the thin asbestos wall, and landed inside. It was straight out of a Bugs Bunny cartoon. That was the moment I retired from testing.

IMAGINATION

My mother taught Sunday school and worked in the kindergarten program at the church across the street. One show-

and-tell day, I had a few scratches on my arm, so when I stood up in front of the class, I explained that they were from an eagle that had swooped down, picked me up, and carried me off to its nest. I told them how I curled up with the other baby birds and ate worms. I even described trying to escape by jumping out of the nest, only to have the eagle dive down and grab me midair and fly me back. Now, I'm pretty sure my mother and the teachers knew this story had some factual weaknesses. But the kids? They were completely spellbound. This was way better than the kid before me talking about his new yo-yo. The scary part is, as I told the story, the more I started to believe it myself. I could see it happening in my head. The details got sharper and more real. I don't know what they call that now—probably something that requires medication—but whatever it was, I had it in spades.

FIRST MUSIC MEMORY

It was a Saturday, school was over for the week, and all I wanted to do was get outside and play. Spring was settling in, the school year was winding down, and the grass was thick and deep green— the kind that felt amazing on bare feet—cool and soft before the calluses of summer had a chance to build up. I was already barefoot, already free, and already headed toward the chicken house where we had just hung a brand-new rope swing that was clearly more important than anything else happening in the world.

That's when I heard my name.

"Tommy, come over here for a minute."

Those words were never good news. They usually meant one of two things: I had either done something wrong, or someone had decided it was time for me to work. Both outcomes ruined a perfectly good Saturday. My instincts screamed, Run!, but experience told me running would only make things worse. My grandma Gibson had apparently decided this was the day she was going to discover whether I had any musical talent. This was not a casual curiosity. She sang in the church choir, and when she sang, you could hear her above everyone else. She had one of those voices that could cut through steel. So, against my will and better judgment, I followed her into the house.

We walked down the hallway to the living room, where the piano lived. Hanging over the fireplace was a painting of the Blue Boy, who I had never trusted. While she dug through the piano bench for sheet music, I stared at him. He had bows on his shoes, a feather in an oversized hat, and what looked like stockings paired with the weirdest shorts I had ever seen. I immediately began praying this was not where the afternoon was headed. If music turned me into that, I wanted no part of it.

She sat down on the piano bench and motioned for me to sit beside her. I sat, though every fiber of my being wanted to bolt for the door.

"I want you to sing the note I play," she said.

She hit a key.

I stared at the piano.

"Come on, Tommy. Just sing the note."

She played the note again.

I still sat there.

This was a problem. I was extremely shy, and I also had no idea what she meant. Sing it how?

Was there a word involved?

Was I supposed to hum?

Moan? Guess?

She played the note again, louder this time, as if volume would help me understand. She was clearly getting irritated. I was clearly not matching the version of this moment she had rehearsed in her head.

"Just sing, 'aw,' Tommy."

So I said, "aw," the way you do when you feel sorry for someone.

"No," she said. "As in singing."

"Don't they sing words, Grandma?"

She paused. This was not the answer she was looking for.

"Just sing the note." She played it again.

I tried. I really did. Unfortunately, I sang every note except the one she played. I wandered so far off pitch I probably discovered notes no one else had ever found. That's when she slammed the piano cover shut, looked at me like a great mystery had been solved, and said, "Well… music may just not be in the cards for you."

I can't say I was devastated. All I could think about was that rope swing waiting for me outside. Ave always had a talent for frustrating people by asking questions that, to them, should have been obvious.

To me, they never were.

Chapter 2

Party Lines, Small Towns, and Other Warning Signs

Every Sunday after dinner, the phone would ring, and it was always my grandparents calling from Scottsville, Virginia.

The call followed a strict chain of command. Dad answered first. He'd talk for a few minutes, usually about when we were coming up to visit next. Then the phone went to Mom.

I never understood why, when a long-distance call came in, my mother felt the need to talk louder. Did she think she had to yell all the way to Scottsville? Was she worried the phone lines couldn't carry her voice that far? Whatever the reason, the volume always went up.

After Mom, the phone moved down the line to my brothers, and finally to me. I was always last. My entire conversation usually consisted of one question: "How's the weather down there?" I'd say something like, "Cold." This would immediately trigger a detailed comparison between the weather in Scottsville and the weather in Virginia Beach—even though they had just asked my brothers the exact same question thirty seconds earlier.

Once the weather had been fully discussed, analyzed,

and compared to previous winters going back to the Eisenhower administration, they wanted to talk to Dad again. That was it.

Call over.

I was officially released back into the wild.

We had a rotary-dial phone, and our number started with GY7—something I won't finish here because my mother still uses the same number. At one point, we even had a party line, which meant another household shared our phone line. If the phone rang in a certain pattern—two short rings, for example—you knew whether it was for you or the other people.

Sometimes—and I'm not proud of this—I'd listen in on the other conversations. There was an old woman on the line who talked nonstop about her bursitis. That and her husband spending too much time in the sheep barn. I heard a lot about both. More than any child should ever hear about either topic.

It turned out these people were neighbors down the street. One Sunday, the elderly man pushed his wife down the stairs, carried her to the car, and turned on the engine to let the fumes take them both in the closed garage. They were discovered a few days later, sitting in their vintage Model T.

After all the commotion died down, I rode my bike over to their house and looked into the garage. The car was still there. I stood staring through the window, trying to understand what could lead someone to do something like that. The car had been painted white with house paint. You could still see the brush marks. It's a strange thing to realize how much weight people carry quietly.

And it's a pity when it finally breaks them.

SCOTTSVILLE

My grandparents and great-grandparents on my father's side moved to Scottsville, Virginia, when I was very young. Scottsville is a small town about twenty miles outside of Charlottesville. At one point, Thomas Jefferson practiced law in the old courthouse there back in the mid-1700s, which already made the place feel important—even if it didn't look like it was trying very hard to prove it.

Scottsville sits on the banks of the James River and was once a major port city for Charlottesville. Before trains, goods were shipped up and down the river on bateaux. Later, a lock system was added—the Kanawha Canal— which ran alongside the James. It was originally proposed by George Washington, which seemed fitting, because in Scottsville, history didn't feel dead. It just felt like it had slowed down and stayed put.

If any town ever resembled Mayberry from *The Andy Griffith Show*, this was it. The mayor, Mr. Arthur Raymond Thacker, was also the town undertaker. He was the skinniest man I had ever seen and reminded me of John Carradine—tall, hollow-eyed, and slightly unsettling.

The town had one stoplight and two main streets. That was it. If you missed your turn, you probably ended up back where you started, whether you wanted to or not.

My grandparents bought an old house there to fix up and retire in. They split it into two living spaces—upstairs and downstairs—each with its own kitchen. It was too hard for my great-grandparents to manage the stairs, so they lived downstairs, and my grandparents lived upstairs. To me, this house was a mansion. It had at least six fireplaces, which in my mind meant it was practically a castle. The house sat on top of a large hill overlooking the James River. A massive front porch with columns stretched across the entire front of the house, and across the river you could see what was said to be Thomas Jefferson's brother's home.

Every night after dinner, weather permitting, we'd sit out on that porch while both sets of grandparents told stories about what life used to be like. I loved those evenings. My imagination would take off, and I'd live inside the moments they described.

My great-grandmother was going senile, and every night she had the exact same conversation.

"My, hasn't that tree grown?"

"Yes, Annie."

"Chester, what are we having for dinner?"

"We already ate."

"Well, have you fed the chickens?"

"We haven't had chickens for two years."

One night she came out onto the porch in a panic, convinced she was going blind. Everything looked foggy. She needed a doctor immediately. What had actually happened was she had put face powder on without taking off her glasses, completely coating the lenses. My grandmother wiped them clean, and you would have thought she'd been healed by the hand of God.

HISTORY, LIVESTOCK, AND OTHER LOCALS

I'd always heard a Civil War battle had been fought on the grounds of the house. My brother Jim even found a buried Civil War mule bit with the Union "U.S." emblem still visible. We donated it to the Scottsville museum, where I assume it still sits. As it turns out, Major General Philip Sheridan's expedition of nearly 10,000 troops had camped on that hill. They didn't fight there—they just stopped long enough to remind the land it had seen worse.

My great-grandfather kept chickens we brought from home, along with pigs named Dot and Clara—after my mother and aunt—a goat, a horse, and a few dogs. This house became the setting for some of my best childhood memories.

We had two neighbors: Miss Bertha and the Cooks. Miss Bertha was an old widow who lived in a small shack she had built herself. She survived on milk from her dairy cows, vegetables from her garden, and sewing work she did for locals. My great-grandfather would pick up her milk every morning, take it into town, and sell it for her. Milk and sewing were her only sources of cash.

She also had a man who worked for her—Mr. Mickey— who was an alcoholic. One day, driving down the dirt road that split between Miss Bertha's place and ours, we saw a pair of shoes laid out neatly on the ground—with a human turd placed squarely between them. We immediately knew it was Mickey. How or why this happened was beyond comprehension. Why the shoes were left behind was a mystery no one even tried to solve.

Some things in Scottsville were better left unexplained.

PARADES AND ONE VERY COMMITTED FEATHER

Fourth of July parades were a tradition. We'd pile into a car, ride downtown, and wait. Waiting was the main event. Eventually, you'd hear it—a school marching band a few blocks away, wildly out of tune and getting louder by degrees. Drums first. Then the band. Then a few tractors. Mr. Thacker riding in a convertible, waving as he knew he'd personally buried half the town. There'd be some livestock. Maybe a couple of cows. One or two people on horseback. Then the fire trucks and the sheriff's car and some tractors. The whole thing lasted about thirty minutes.

Afterward, we'd go back to the house for a cookout. My grandfather always pushed the hot dogs, even though everyone clearly preferred hamburgers. He acted like hot dogs were patriotic and hamburgers were suspiciously un-American.

Mrs. Cook was always part of the founding pageant. She dressed as a Native American, wearing a brown dress, colored beads, and a headband with exactly one feather sticking straight up. She also wore cat-rim glasses and kept a cigarette permanently hanging from her mouth. She chain-smoked. This was not exactly my vision of Pocahontas. She laughed constantly—a deep, wheezy, smoker laugh—and was always canning something. If you saw her, something had just been canned, was being canned, or was about to be canned.

Looking back, that parade pretty much summed up Scottsville: history, tradition, livestock, smoke, and one feather doing a lot of heavy lifting.

HONDAS AND POOR JUDGMENT

My uncle had just bought a Honda 50cc motorcycle from a friend who had been renting it down at the beach. It was old and a little beat up, but it ran great—which, as far as we were concerned, made it perfect. Not long after that, he bought another Honda 50cc and then a Trail 90—the one with the low gears made for riding through the woods. He left all of them for us to ride. This was both incredibly generous and wildly irresponsible.

The Continental Can Company owned miles of land nearby, with dirt roads cut through the woods for timber harvesting. For us, it was paradise. We rode those motorcycles constantly—through the trees, down to the railroad tracks, and along them for miles like we owned the place.

One night in June, a terrible storm rolled through. The kind of storm that rattles the house and makes sleep uneasy. The next morning, when we woke up, you could tell something wasn't right. The air felt off. The world looked different. Naturally, we hopped on the bikes. We rode down toward the railroad tracks and into town. There was a bridge there with markers showing how high the river was supposed to be. The water had risen fast—way higher than it should have been. Even we knew that wasn't normal. We turned around and rode as fast as we could back down the tracks, trying to reach the turnoff before the water overtook them. We barely made it. Not long after, the flooding hit hard. That was the big one. The whole town took damage.

Looking back, it's amazing how often our childhood adventures ended with some version of, "We probably shouldn't have been there."

But at the time, it just felt like another ride.

Chapter 3

____

Field Trips, Moats, and the Slow-Motion Train Wreck of Becoming a Musician

School and I never really got along. I didn't like getting up early, and teachers always seemed personally committed to embarrassing me. Nothing struck fear into my heart quite like hearing, "Tommy, come up to the blackboard," which really meant, "Please come allow me to humiliate you in front of your classmates like we're doing a live demonstration of panic." Teachers acted like it was character-building. Which is what adults say when they're about to do something that would get them punched if the roles were reversed.

I was a slow reader and a slow thinker. I needed time to sit with a question and consider all the possibilities. As it turns out, I had dyslexia, though no one figured that out until I was an adult. Back then, you weren't dyslexic—you were "not applying yourself," which is an impressive diagnosis considering no one had any clue what was going on inside your head. Why teachers took such pride in putting kids on the spot in front of a room full of other kids was always beyond me. If you want to watch somebody's soul leave their body, you don't need a Ouija board. You just need a chalkboard and a seventh grade audience.

But every now and then, school accidentally did something right.

It let you leave.

FIELD TRIP

One year, our class went on a field trip to Williamsburg and Yorktown. Williamsburg was about an hour and a half away, and we traveled in one of those yellow school buses with bench seats. There were no seat belts back then—just steel bars you could grab in case of an accident, which pretty much guaranteed you'd lose your teeth if anything went wrong. Adults called it "safety." What it really was was a rolling can of children.

The bus was loud, hot, and smelled like peanut butter, pencils, and bad decisions. The boys acted like they'd been released from prison. The girls sat there looking like they were already tired of us, which was fair. I would scan the bus for an empty seat and quietly hope a girl would sit next to me. It wasn't that I had anything against boys—it was just easier to talk to girls. With boys, there was always the risk of saying something wrong and getting punched, or worse, being called a sissy for having a thought. I always liked girls because you could talk without it becoming a sport. Most of the boys treated conversation like a boxing match: you either won, lost, or ran.

My mother had given me money to buy a souvenir. This was supposed to be educational. The other kids came back with pottery, blown glass, copies of the Constitution, and those three-cornered Revolutionary War hats—the ones that make every child look like a tiny tax collector. I returned with a giant cigar and a small silver lighter shaped like a pistol. Which tells you everything you need to know about my priorities.

I would later burn down the field next to my grandparents' house playing with that lighter. This wasn't intentional. It was curiosity. And also because I was apparently born with an inner voice that said, "Let's see what happens."

The cigar was about the size of a deli pickle. When I got home, I sat in the ditch that ran through our front yard and tried to smoke it like I'd just returned from a hard day at the shipyard. It tasted awful. I kept going anyway, because at that age you're not smoking for flavor. You're smoking for the idea of smoking. I eventually cut it open and discovered it was filled with sawdust. So apparently the only real culture I picked up on that trip came from a cigar filled with sawdust.

Despite everything, I loved field trips. You got out of school for an entire day, which alone made them worth it. I would usually grab a seat, but most often, the person I absolutely didn't want sitting there would plop down beside me and start talking nonstop. I'd just stare out the window, watching the world go by, daydreaming about flying or going back in time—anywhere but the blackboard. Anywhere but a teacher saying, "Tommy ... explain your answer," while my brain did what it always did under pressure:

Leave the building.

COTTAGE NEXT DOOR

Our neighbors, the Mumfords, owned the land on either side of our property. They had three small rental cottages behind their house. Which meant, in practical terms, that we were surrounded. The Mumfords were not particularly fond of us boys. They never wanted us on their land, and on any given day, you could hear Mrs. Mumford yelling at someone for trespassing—usually us. I had visions of her spending her entire day running from window to window, just waiting for one of us to jump the ditch so she could start screaming—like an air-raid siren with curtains.

Our three acres were bordered by ditches, so unless you went out through the driveway, jumping a ditch was how you got anywhere. To me, the ditches were a moat, and we were English royalty defending the castle. Which is hilarious, because we were about as royal as a bag of feed. In spring, when it rained hard, the ditches filled to the top. You could float toy boats (sticks) for a long way. I took this seriously. I had naval ambitions. We had fleets. We had missions. We had deep emotional investment in whether a stick could make it around the bend without capsizing. The truth is, the ditch was one of the best parts of our childhood. It was a border, a battlefield, a highway, and occasionally a place to sit and think when you didn't understand people.

One summer evening, I stepped outside and heard a sound drifting through the air. An electric guitar, boogieing away. It stopped me in my tracks. I followed the sound and saw one of the tenants in those rental cottages sitting on his porch with a small amp and an electric guitar. He had slicked-back hair with duck tails and was leaning back in a wooden chair, balanced on two legs against the wall like he'd been doing it his whole life. I had to see this up close.

Now, this was tricky. The cottages belonged to the Mumfords, and they already hated us. That hatred had intensified after they opened a bar across the street, and my mother, grandmother, and a few neighbors started a petition to have it shut down—and won. Not exactly how you build a strong community bond.

Still, there was that ditch separating our properties, and I crossed it anyway. The moat had failed. The castle was compromised. The guy looked at me and said, "Hey, kid, you know about Elvis?"

"Sure," I said. "I saw him on *The Ed Sullivan Show*." That did it. He sat up straight and launched into "You Ain't Nothin' But a Hound Dog." He went from song to song without saying much. We didn't really have a conversation. I just stood there watching him play, completely locked in.

Somewhere in the background, I could hear my mother yelling for me to come in for supper. I ignored her. This wasn't rebellion. This was discovery. I stood there about half an hour until the neighbors finally ran me off, and even then I didn't leave willingly. I left because you can only trespass so long before someone decides to add "discipline" to the evening schedule. It was the coolest thing I had ever seen.

From that moment on, I needed to be around music. I loved the way it made me feel. I started searching it out wherever I could find it. It didn't matter what kind of music it was—I just wanted to watch people play. There was a small Black Baptist church not far from our house, and on Sunday mornings I would sit outside just to listen to the choir. The sound was joyful and alive, nothing like the stiff, drowning music at my church. It never even occurred to me to go inside. I wasn't avoiding it. It just didn't feel like I belonged. So I sat outside where nobody could tell me to come to the blackboard and prove I deserved to be there.

KENT GUITAR

We went over to my Uncle Kenny's house one day, and my cousins had a cousin visiting at the same time. He showed up with a brand-new Kent guitar strung with flatwound strings. I had never seen anything so beautiful in my life. I couldn't wait to get my hands on it. The tone was incredible

—warm and smooth—and I remember getting into a fistfight with my brother over who got to hold it. Not play it. Hold it. That's how serious this was.

As it turned out, the whole gathering was set up so my brother could start a band with him. My father was an amateur jazz drummer in his spare time, and he had taught my brother how to play. Jim was really good. He'd been playing since he was little, and it showed. The idea of a band completely blew my mind. I wanted in. Badly.

There was only one small problem:

I didn't play anything.

Music was starting to change around that time. The Beatles had "I Want to Hold Your Hand" on the radio, and I was getting pulled in deeper and deeper. The sounds were new, different, and they spoke to me in a way nothing else ever had. I loved listening to the radio—all of it. Rock, pop, whatever came on. There were so many styles, so many sounds, and I wanted all of them.

There was a song called "Little Black Egg" by the Nightcrawlers that was getting airplay. My cousin's cousin knew how to play it. That stopped me cold. It had never occurred to me that you could learn something you heard on the radio. Not just listen to it—but make it yourself. The song was simple, but I loved it. The sound, the feel, the fact that it existed at all. He showed me how to play it. And that was it. Something clicked. I begged my parents for a guitar. They agreed—but only if I took lessons. I didn't care. I was thrilled. Lessons? Fine. Whatever it took. Then it hit me. Lessons meant homework. And I hated homework. Why was everything I loved always starting to feel like school?

FIRST GUITAR

My first guitar was a Silvertone from Sears. The strings
were so high off the fretboard I could barely make a chord.
My fingers would bleed after I finished practicing, but that
didn't matter. I had to learn. If that's what it took, then
that's what I was going to do. It was really more of a toy
than a guitar. An acoustic with a sunburst finish, straight
out of the Sears catalog. It sat just one step above the model
with the Roy Rogers logo and the sheriff's star—you know,
the one with the string for a guitar strap. So technically, I
had upgraded.

I bought a book of chords and learned them two at a
time so I could practice changing between them. That was
the plan: two chords, over and over, until my fingers either
learned or fell off. I really wanted an electric. But it didn't
matter. It was a box with strings, and for the first time I was
starting to figure some things out. And that was enough to
keep me going.

LESSONS

I was supposed to take lessons from Mr. Griggs at the
Griggs School of Music, and I couldn't wait. I even put new
strings on my guitar. The only problem was: I had watched
Elvis on *The Ed Sullivan Show* the night before, and he had
left the ends of his strings hanging loose from the headstock.
Naturally, I decided this was the coolest thing I had ever
seen and that my guitar should look exactly like that. We
pulled up in front of the building, and I jumped out of the
car, grabbed my guitar—no case, just raw guitar—and ran
inside full of excitement. The very first thing Mr. Griggs
said was, "We need to cut those strings off. They could poke
your eye out." He completely ignored the cool factor.

I asked him if he could play something. He picked up a guitar and played a little boogie number, and just like that, I was hooked again. *Okay*, I thought. *This guy knows something.* Then he pulled out a sheet of beginner music and placed it in front of me. This was not what I had in mind. I thought he was going to teach me guitar—not enroll me in reading class. He pointed to the staff and started explaining Every Good Boy Does Fine and FACE. I stared at the page, wondering what any of this had to do with the Beatles or Elvis. Sheet music looked like birds sitting on telephone wires. It made absolutely no sense to me. Then he said, "We're going to start with—"

Please say "Johnny B. Goode."

"—'Twinkle, Twinkle, Little Star.'"

I was devastated. "Twinkle, Twinkle, Little Star?" *Are you kidding me?* There was a whole world of music happening right now, and he was teaching me bedtime songs. Why were we wasting time with nursery rhymes when the Beatles were rewriting history and Elvis was shaking the nation into a moral crisis?

This went on for maybe three lessons, and then I quit. I decided maybe I wasn't meant to play music—maybe I was just meant to be a fan. So I became a serious one.

VINYL

I started buying albums—albums being large, round black plastic discs with grooves in them—and talking to anyone who would listen about what they were into and who was making new music. I loved the smell of a new LP the moment you tore open the plastic and slid out the sleeve. I loved the ritual: the careful handling, the reading of liner notes like they were scripture, the moment the needle dropped and those first scratchy sounds came alive. It wasn't just music. It felt like distant worlds opening up. It was the first time I realized there might be a life beyond my little one.

The first LP I remember buying was Bob Dylan's 1962 album. What pulled me in wasn't even the music at first—it was the back cover. It read like a book, full of stories about Dylan and his influences, and I was curious. When I finally heard "You're No Good," I was hooked. This sound was nothing like what I heard on the radio. It felt older. Stranger. Like it came from another time and place. Immediately, I decided I wanted to be a hobo. That was it. I'd ride the rails, see the country, eat out of tuna cans, and swap stories with other hobos. I imagined myself with a stick slung over my shoulder, a bag tied to the end. Maybe I'd find an old stray dog to travel with. He could keep me company, and we could keep each other warm at night. In my mind, I had found my calling. I was going to be a singing bum. There was nothing more noble than that as far as I was concerned. There was just one small problem: There were no trains around, and I wasn't allowed to cross the street.

THINGS CHANGE

Around this time, I started to notice things changing. My older brothers were getting into music, and just being around them exposed me to more than I would have found on my own. There was an uneasiness in the air. Even as a kid, you could feel it. The television was filled with news of riots, war protests, and civil rights marches. We still had segregated schools in Virginia, and I had very little exposure to Black people. But I was captivated by their music—even then. The joy in gospel. The heart-wrenching sorrow of the blues. To me, this was music that came from somewhere deeper—music meant to soothe a hard life. And once I heard it, I knew I wanted to follow it. Wherever it led.

Seventh grade was when life really started to change for me. The innocence I had known began to fade away, though not gracefully. The first day of school was pure awkwardness. By then I was almost six feet tall and weighed about 140 pounds. If I walked past a row of corn stalks, you would've sworn we were related. My voice had decided to go off on its own adventure. One minute it was deep and rich, the next it shot up into high squeaks without warning. Sometimes it wouldn't even let me finish a word before going rogue. Everything was embarrassing—my clothes, my body, the fact that I towered over most of the other kids. I just wanted to crawl into a hole and stay there.

My parents expected me to ride the school bus, but honestly, I didn't fit. My legs were too long for the seats and jammed into the aluminum backing in front of me. Every time the driver hit the brakes, it felt like punishment. I was fine as long as I didn't have to share a seat, but the bus was always packed. Comfort and dignity were not options.

I wanted to be cool. I wanted to be accepted. Unfortunately, I had absolutely no idea how to do either of those things.

Which, looking back, explains a lot.

Chapter 4

Evan, or How I Learned That Music Saves You and Drugs Do Not

I met Evan in seventh grade, which was right around the time my body decided to grow six feet tall while my confidence stayed about four inches. I towered over most of the other kids and had no idea what to do with that fact. I was painfully shy, awkward, and still trying to figure out how conversations worked. Evan, on the other hand, had already figured out life—or at least looked like he had. He was husky, popular, and had a reputation as a badass and a fighter. Just sitting next to him in class made me nervous. I didn't talk to him at first. I wasn't sure what the rules were, and I had already learned that guessing wrong could hurt. He was best friends with another kid named Mike.

One day, out of nowhere, Evan asked me what I had done over the summer. He told me he had gotten some pussy. I told him we didn't get a cat. That should have been the end of the conversation. The friendship should have died right there, buried under confusion and bad timing. Somehow, it didn't. What saved me was music. And surfing. Next to music, surfing was my favorite thing in the world. Evan told me he was building a surfboard. I told him I was building one too. That was it. No background checks. No interviews. We were friends. I learned early that shared obsession is stronger than personality.

HITCHHIKING (OR, HOW I SURVIVED THE SIXTIES)

By that point, I was hitchhiking to get around. Back then, that was just something people did. You stuck your thumb out and hoped for the best. I only ran into serious trouble three times. Once, a pervert tried to have his way with me, but I jumped out of the car at the first red light. Another time, a car full of guys pulled a knife on me and robbed me. They got fifty cents and a pack of cigarettes. I was so nervous I asked if I could have one of my cigarettes back. They dumped me out of the car and sped off. The third time, a guy pulled a gun, pressed it to my temple, and told me he'd just been released from prison. When he started slowing down and pulling off the road, I jumped out of the moving car and ran into the woods. Anyway, I made it to Evan's house and knocked on the door.

THE ADDAMS FAMILY, VIRGINIA BEACH EDITION

Evan's mother answered wearing only a bra and panties. If you're imagining a beautiful young woman, stop. This was not that situation. I didn't know where I was supposed to look, so I chose the ground.

"Is Evan home?" I asked.

"I think so. Come on in." She walked into the living room and opened what I thought was a closet—it had clothes hanging in it—and yelled inside, "Evan!" At this point, I was pretty sure I had wandered into the Addams

Family house. A few minutes later, strange noises came from inside the wall, and Evan appeared out of the closet.

"Come on up," he said, then disappeared back inside. It turned out the "closet" was actually a staircase with a door. His mother hung clothes in it to take upstairs.

He had an old reel-to-reel tape machine up there. Evan was listening to Donovan. At some point, he had melted a candle and dripped wax onto the tape reel, permanently attaching it. This should have been a warning sign.

LSD, OR THE LONGEST NIGHT OF MY LIFE

We stayed friends until the day Evan put LSD in my milk and didn't tell me. I remember going into his bathroom and looking in the mirror when suddenly my face turned into a pig's face. Then everything started leaving trails. Then I felt like I could travel through time. Nothing made sense. Everything terrified me. I didn't know what was happening. I just wanted it to stop. Evan laughed and said, "Enjoy the trip." His brother Mitch finally took me home and let me out of the car because I was completely losing it. I kept thinking, *Please, please, let this end.* I was terrified it would be permanent. It lasted twelve hours. It felt like I had gone to hell and couldn't leave. I curled up in a ball, shaking, waiting for it to pass. I hated every second of it. That was it for me. I never wanted another drug in my body again.

What I didn't know then was that I'd be dealing with the effects of that night for the rest of my life. Evan started using heroin by fifteen. He was dead by twenty-one. He died on his twenty-first birthday, hollowed out, jumping from a moving car and hitting a telephone pole. What a waste. To this day, when I hear people talk about how cool drugs are, I want to run the other way. There is nothing cool about absolute hell.

PANIC

About a week later, the panic attacks started. If you've never had one, it's hard to explain. Words don't really work. Mine usually began in the middle of the night. I'd wake up feeling like I couldn't breathe. My heart would be racing, my body buzzing, and I'd be convinced the LSD trip was starting all over again. That was the worst part—the fear that it had come back. And then something strange happened: I became afraid of the fear itself. That's when the cycle starts. You panic. Then you panic because you're panicking. Then you panic about whether this is permanent. Around and around it goes, faster each time.

I had never heard the terms panic attack or anxiety. All I knew was that something was very wrong, and I honestly believed I was going crazy. I tried talking to my mother. She laughed and said, "What problems could you possibly have at your age?"

That shut the door pretty quickly.

So I kept it to myself. There were moments when I thought, *If this doesn't stop, I can't live like this.* I didn't want to die. I just wanted the fear to end. At one point, it felt like there were only two options: keep going like this forever, or not go on at all. I needed something to live for. Music turned out to be that thing.

Around the same time, I became very spiritual. I remember praying—not for myself to be spared, but asking God not to let other people feel what I was feeling. I wouldn't have wished it on anyone. The panic didn't disappear overnight. It took years. But music gave me somewhere to put the fear when everything else felt unreal. Sometimes, that was enough to get me through the night.

SCHOOL (STILL THE ENEMY)

God, I hated school. There was nothing I hated more. I spent most of my childhood feeling stupid, and school made sure I never forgot it. Teachers were always telling me I wasn't living up to my potential. That phrase followed me everywhere. And I always wondered—how in the hell would they know that? What exactly was my potential, and when did they become experts on it? I didn't learn the way they wanted me to learn. I needed time. I needed space. I didn't arrive at answers the fastest, but I arrived at them honestly.

Spelling was the worst. I am terrible at spelling. Always have been. Always will be. I often thought they should put misspelled words on my gravestone. Maybe one of my schoolteachers would walk by and try to figure out how to correct something carved in granite. In school, spelling wasn't just a skill—it was a judgment. Misspell a word and suddenly it wasn't that you spelled the word wrong, it was *you* were wrong. I never once looked at someone struggling to make a G chord and thought, *What an idiot.* I understood that some things take time. Some things hurt your fingers. So maybe—just maybe—people should shut the hell up about things they don't understand. You never know what someone is dealing with. You don't know how their brain works. You don't know what's happening behind the scenes. All you see is the moment they fall short of your expectations.

For years, I thought I was stupid because school told me I was. It wasn't until much later that I learned there was a name for what I had. I wasn't broken. I just didn't fit the mold.

BROTHERS, BANDS, AND BELONGING

My middle brother Jim was a drummer, and when he got into high school, he put together a band. I lived for rehearsal nights. Watching amps get dragged across the floor and guitars come out of cases felt ceremonial—like something important was about to happen. The guitar player had a black Rickenbacker. Even then, I knew it was special. That sound stays with you.

One of the songs they were doing required two guitars, and Berkeley, the bass player, showed me a simple bass line to play for the song. And suddenly, I was in. The first time we started playing together, something happened that I had never felt before. It wasn't just sound—it was movement. The drums pushed, the guitars floated on top, and the bass sat right in the middle, locking everything together. You could feel the music physically, like it had weight and momentum. When everyone hit the same beat at the same time, it felt like the room snapped into focus. My timing wasn't great. I was late, early, and occasionally just wrong. But nobody stopped. Nobody pointed it out. The song kept going. That was the magic. In that moment, I wasn't awkward. I wasn't shy. I wasn't the kid who hated school. I was necessary. I was a Beatle. And once you feel that—once you disappear into a song with other people—there's no going back.

WOODSTOCK FROM A DIRT PILE

There was a drive-in movie theater about two miles down the street from our house. It sat behind a brand-new grocery store that had just been built, and the construction company had left behind a big mound of dirt. To us, that dirt pile might as well have been reserved seating. From the top of that hill, you could see right over the fence and watch the movies for free. That's where I saw *Woodstock*. I must've watched it four times in two weeks. The sound was terrible, drifting in from car speakers, but it didn't matter. I filled in the rest in my head.

It felt like a glimpse into another way of living. A place where music wasn't entertainment, it was a language. A gathering point. A shield.

Around that time, I realized the innocence I'd been carrying was gone. I started having this strange, unsettling thought that in just a few years I might be going to war in Vietnam—and that I might not come home. It wasn't abstract. It felt very real. I had friends whose older brothers had gone off to war and never returned. One world told you who to be. The other asked why. I didn't have answers yet. I just knew music was somehow going to be part of how I survived.

FLETCHER

Evan's older brother, Fletcher, ran away from home and went to Woodstock. To me, that made him a legend. When I finally talked to him, I learned he'd done so many drugs and drank so much that he passed out in the mud for most of it. That was it. No revelations. No epiphanies. It was my first lesson in the difference between the idea of something and the reality of it. I didn't want the drugs. I didn't want the chaos. I wanted the music. That realization didn't kill the dream. It clarified it. And that made all the difference.

Chapter 5

Don't Play Music: A Cautionary Tale That Didn't Work

I know my family meant well, but they always seemed vaguely disappointed that I wanted to play music. Not angry—just that quiet, heavy disappointment that makes you feel like you've chosen a life of mild embarrassment.

My father used to tell me to quit plunking around on the guitar and go out into the world and do something useful. That always confused me. What exactly was I supposed to do? Most of the jobs I could imagine held absolutely no appeal. I didn't dream of climbing ladders, wearing ties, or being promoted to assistant something. I only wanted one thing—to be a musician—and I couldn't understand why that seemed so unrealistic to everyone else. Other people were doing it. Some of them were even getting rich doing it. So why not me?

School was exhausting. Who wants to read about life when you could actually be out living it? I never understood why curiosity was supposed to end at the classroom door. That felt backward. People's opinions didn't matter much to me then, and they still don't. If you truly love something, you don't really get a choice—you have to pursue it. Ignoring that pull feels worse than failing.

It seems to me that most of us spend our lives trying to fit in. We search for communities that agree with our ideas and beliefs, hoping that belonging will give our lives meaning and justify who we are. Somewhere along the way, it becomes perfectly acceptable to tear down anyone who doesn't line up with our thinking. We all say we're individuals, but we're constantly looking for approval to prove it. We become like pets—willing to do almost anything for attention.

I never really fit anywhere. I wanted to, badly. But I thought differently, and I learned early on to keep that to myself. I didn't want to follow a crowd. I wanted to come to my own conclusions about life, even if that meant standing alone for a while. Henry Ford was once asked if he listened to what customers wanted. He said if he had, they would've asked for a faster horse. That always stuck with me. America used to celebrate individuals. Somehow, we started celebrating agreement instead. Pick a side. Stay there. No middle ground.

Creativity is a beautiful thing, but it's almost never accepted until the masses decide it's popular. Until then, it's treated like a nuisance—something people tolerate as long as it doesn't get too loud or ask for money. I can't count how many times people have told me what direction I should take my music. It took me a long time to realize there was only one direction it could go—out of me. That was it. Anything else would've been dishonest. I was never especially gifted as a singer or a musician. That just wasn't in the cards. What I was drawn to was songwriting. That's what I wanted to do, and that's what I set out to become. Along the way, I learned to play a lot of different instruments—not great at any one of them, but good enough to serve the song. And in the end, that was all I ever wanted to do anyway.

RAMBLING CONRADS

Across the street from Old Dominion University in Norfolk, Virginia, there was a small guitar shop called Rambling Conrads. It specialized in acoustic guitars and smelled like wood, sweat, and dreams that hadn't been crushed yet.

On weekend nights, they'd drag out folding chairs and host open mic nights. The shop was tiny—guitars hanging on every wall, barely any floor space, and a small side room in the back with a drink machine and the bathrooms. That back room was where you prepared to go onstage. You tuned your guitar, tried not to throw up, and questioned every decision you'd ever made. It wasn't a dressing room. Hell, I was already dressed.

Bob, the owner, ran the whole thing. He had a sign-up sheet. First to sign up, first to play. No hiding. No easing into it. No "maybe later." That's where I was about to have my very first stage experience. Driving to Rambling Conrads that night, I almost turned around at every inter-section. Every red light felt like an opportunity to escape. I tried singing in the car to warm up my voice. I was never a gifted singer, but if you're a songwriter, singing is part of the deal whether you like it or not. At that point in my life, I had a deep fondness for Ramblin' Jack Elliott. What I loved about him was that he wasn't a great singer either—but the way he turned a phrase pulled you right into the song. It felt real. When he sang, you were suddenly there with him. Freight trains, wide open land, and a time much harder than anything I'd ever lived through. I decided I would pattern myself after him. The only problem was I hadn't mastered his phrasing, so what came out of me sounded more like garbled hoots and groans.

I sat in the back room waiting for my name to be called. My palms were sweating, my mouth was bone-dry, and I was pretty sure I might pass out. I listened to the other performers, and some of them were really good. This did not help. When Bob finally called my name, every instinct in my body told me to run. Instead, I walked toward the stage—which, for the record, was just a stool in the corner of the room. I sat down and introduced myself, then immediately realized I had forgotten to use the restroom. So I stood up, walked into the back room, used the bathroom, came back out, put money into the drink machine, and got a soda. You could hear the can clunk its way down through the machine. People laughed. I'm pretty sure they heard the toilet flush too. I returned to the stage, sat on the stool, leaned back—and promptly fell off. At this point, I wanted the earth to open up and swallow me whole. Somehow, the audience thought this was intentional. Like it was part of the act. I played my two songs, barely remembering how they went, and slinked off the stage. I packed up my guitar, got to my car, and sat there cycling through a full range of emotions—from *I should never show my face in public again* to *I kind of want to do that again.* By the time I got home, I knew the answer. I wanted to go back. I wanted to learn how to work a crowd. I wanted to figure out how to entertain people. And eventually, I wanted to learn how to stay on the stool. It's hard to explain why someone who's shy and hates speaking in front of people would choose this as a way of life. But I did. And once you step onto a stage—even terrified—you don't really forget how it feels.

BLUEGRASS AND TASSELS

A friend asked if I could fill in for his guitar player in a blue-grass band. He said he had a gig and really needed the money. I said sure. I didn't ask many questions. This was my first mistake. The gig turned out to be at a strip club. We did not go over well. Why the owner thought this was a good idea is still a mystery. The place was packed with horny rednecks who were there to see strippers—not a bunch of long-haired kids playing dueling banjos. It was like someone had confused two completely separate mailing lists. I can still picture the place clearly: bright blue and red lights glowing in a dingy, smoke-filled room, the smell of cheap beer hanging in the air, and the sharp click of high heels on the hardwood stage.

We had to wait for the first dancer to finish her routine before we could go on. She circled a pole and leaned back as far as humanly possible while holding on. This club required the dancers to wear pasties—with tassels. At one point, she got both tassels spinning in different directions. I have questions. When do you discover you can do that? Is there practice involved? Do you wake up one morning thinking, *I might have a future in rotational nipple accessories?*

The crowd went wild. She finished, smiled sweetly, and said, "Your turn, boys." So we stumbled onto the stage and, against all logic, positioned ourselves around the pole. I don't remember who started yelling first, but it wasn't the usual "we don't like your music" kind of yelling. It was more along the lines of "get off the stage or we are going to kill you" yelling. Things got scary fast. After that, the strippers came back out—apparently feeling sorry for us. Suddenly we had banjos and boobs sharing the same space. I stood there playing while tassels spun inches from my face to the sound of bluegrass. It felt like being trapped inside someone else's deeply confusing redneck dream. We were never invited back. As a matter of fact, we didn't even finish the night. And that was my brief career as a bluegrass musician in a strip club.

THE FIRST PA

At some point, I decided if I was going to do this for real, I needed a PA. That felt like the dividing line between messing around and committing. There was a local store called Audio Light & Music that carried Peavey gear, and they had a setup I wanted so badly it almost hurt. It cost around a thousand dollars, which at the time might as well have been a million.

I'd go in and just stand there staring at it. I already had my first real acoustic guitar—a Guild—and now my attention had shifted. I was convinced that if I had that PA, everything else would fall into place. Most places you played didn't have PA systems. You were expected to bring your own. And I hated bad sound. Nothing killed a song faster than a dull, lifeless PA.

So I came up with a plan. I would ask my father to co-sign a loan. This is where the plan became fragile. My dad was a fireman. He wasn't thrilled with my musical ambitions, which was confusing considering he played drums and filled in with jazz bands. But to him, that was a hobby. Music wasn't something you bet your future on. To a lot of people his age, we were just long-haired, pot-smoking hippies who cared about neither God nor country. In my mind, I was a surfer who thought he was Woody Guthrie. Eventually, I worked up the nerve and asked him. He sat me down and gave me a lecture on responsibility. He told me if I missed a payment, it would land squarely on his

shoulders—and he couldn't afford that. I told him I understood. I promised I'd be responsible. I meant it. After a long
pause, he signed the note. That moment felt huge. I walked
out of there feeling like the world had just opened up. I had
a PA. I had a Guild guitar. And I had a 1966 Barracuda
fastback with a slant-six engine. As far as I was concerned, I
had everything I needed. What more could I possibly want?

Chapter 6

Washington, D.C. (or How I Briefly Became Homeless on Purpose)

I wanted to go somewhere I didn't know anybody. Somewhere I could grow musically. Somewhere I wasn't already locked into being that guy everyone thought they understood. I'd been reading about how Dylan just took off for New York City to chase his music, and I figured it was time for me to do the same. Maybe not New York—but somewhere bigger than home. Somewhere with energy. Somewhere you could feel ideas moving around in the air. So I packed up my Barracuda and headed toward Washington, D.C. By then, I had already figured out how to live out of that car. The backseat folded down into a bed, which I'd used plenty of times on surf trips—sleeping in campgrounds, parking lots, and places that probably didn't want me there. The rear window on a 1966 Barracuda fastback was long and curved, all glass.

One time, on a surf trip to the Outer Banks, I got out of the car in the morning and realized I'd left a perfect imprint of my bare ass on that window. I always liked sleeping in the buff. That imprint stayed there for a few days. I thought it was funny. It felt like a signature. Like I was marking territory no one had asked me to claim.

So off I went, convinced I could live in my car and make
my way in the world.

COUCHES, GUITARS, AND STRATEGIC PARKING

My friend Mike had joined the Army and was stationed
just outside D.C. in Leesburg, Virginia, working as a
recruiter's assistant. He let me sleep on his couch for a few
weeks. That was the plan—if you can call it that. There was
a bar in town with an open mic night, and I became a regu-
lar. When I ran out of couch time, I started parking my car
at the houses of people I'd met and sleeping there instead.
This was less a housing strategy and more a game of musical
chairs. Eventually, I met a guy named Ron who told me I
could get a job cutting grass at a girls' school in Middleburg,
Virginia, called Foxcroft. His father ran security there. It
didn't pay much. But they had rooms over the garage where
you could live. And they fed you. That last part sealed it.

FOXCROFT: WEALTH, POWER, AND BACKGROUND CHECKS

Foxcroft was not your average school. It was for the ultra-
wealthy. The kind of wealthy that doesn't talk loudly and
never checks price tags. One day, I was called into the office
and told they were doing a background check on me
because graduation was coming up and some "important
people" would be attending. This was confusing, considering my most recent address was "wherever the Barracuda
fits." On graduation day, Rolls-Royces started pulling in.
Secret Service agents were everywhere—earpieces, suits,
scanning the horizon like an assassination attempt was
imminent. The grounds staff was permitted to observe the

ceremony from a raised vantage point overlooking a grassy amphitheater with a stage in front where the students were seated.

I was standing there when Jackie Onassis walked up and stopped right beside me. She dropped her purse, and some of her things spilled onto the ground. I froze. I was afraid if I bent down to help her, the Secret Service would shoot me. She bent down, picked everything up herself, stood, and gave me a look that could cut glass. What stuck with me wasn't the look. It was her eyes. It felt like someone had scooped the soul right out of her. She was physically there—but the lights were off. That stayed with me.

THE CELLAR DOOR AND BECOMING A SONGWRITER

Washington did something to me. It's where I really fell into folk music. There was a club called the Cellar Door, and in my mind, it became holy ground. Tom Rush, Jackson Browne, and James Taylor had all played there. I wanted to play there as well. One day, I drove into D.C. with my guitar, talked my way into the manager's office, and played him a song. He let me open for a local act that night. The room was small—but it mattered.

It was then that I realized my true passion lay in songwriting. While I lacked a remarkable voice, songs didn't care about that. They simply sought honesty in my lyrics. I bought spiral notebooks and started writing whatever came into my head. I went through notebook after notebook. I fell in love with artists who could take you somewhere else for three minutes and leave you changed. I'd written my first song that year. I only remember one verse now:

The pope, he stands impatient with his silver and his cloth,

Frowning at starvation, but not willing to yield its cost.
For kneeling in the gutter where hobos often lay,
Is bound to break nobility and the crown in which he's paid.

Words have always been jumbled in my head. Getting them out wasn't easy. But once they were on paper, they felt real—like I had proof I existed.

I loved being in D.C. It felt like the center of the universe. People in coffee shops talking about the world and what was happening to it. My generation was forcing change, and I wanted to be part of it.

DYLAN, FIRE, AND A NUDE MISTAKE

In 1974, Bob Dylan and The Band played at the Capital Centre. That night lit a fire in me that never went out. After that show, I couldn't think about anything else. Total tunnel vision. I didn't want fame. I didn't want pop nonsense. I wanted to write music that mattered. I thought I was exactly where I was supposed to be. Which is usually when life steps in.

I lost my job at Foxcroft. I had met a woman at a club where I was playing and invited her back to my room over the garage. This was strictly against the rules. Everything was fine—until morning. She decided to stand nude in front of the window and smoke a cigarette. That window over-looked the parking lot where the guys I worked with gathered every morning. Instead of going inside, they pulled out folding chairs and sat there watching her. I knew immediately this was not going to end well. I was called into the dean's office and asked to explain why she was there. There really wasn't much to explain. I was fired on the spot. A few days later, I packed up and headed back to Virginia Beach. It felt like a step backward. It wasn't.

THE JEWISH MOTHER

Back home, a friend told me about a deli opening on Pacific Avenue called The Jewish Mother. They were looking for musicians. I went to a party to meet the guy booking talent. This was my first real exposure to a gay man who was fully comfortable being himself. I was…not. He ran up, bumped his hip into mine, put his hands in my hair, and squealed, "Oh my God, I love this color." I froze. Eventually, he said, "I'll give you the job because you're cute." Then he asked if I was gay. I said no. He replied, "What a waste of a man."

I became the first of the acts to play there. The hours were ten p.m. to two a.m. You got free food. They had the best hot pastrami I'd ever eaten. I'd play for forty-five minutes, take a fifteen-minute break, flirt with the waitress, then do it all over again until closing.

The Jewish Mother quickly turned into a hangout for musicians. Local players, traveling acts—anyone passing through town usually ended up there late at night.

One night while I was playing, Joe Vannelli—Gino Vannelli's brother—came in. His band sat in with me. Joe noticed I was doing a lot of my own songs and suggested I meet Gino to talk about writing together. They were playing at Chrysler Hall in Norfolk, and Joe gave me tickets. I was supposed to meet them at the mixing console after the show. Gino had a hit at the time and was clearly on his way up. I went to the concert. I left before the meeting. I just didn't feel like we were heading in the same direction. Later, I realized his direction was success—and mine wasn't. At least not in the conventional sense. I wanted to go my own way. I didn't want anyone telling me what I should be doing.

Surf during the day. Music at night. That felt like winning.

RED MULE AND ALMOST BEING SOMEBODY

I started playing at a place in Norfolk called the Red Mule. The first time I went there, it wasn't to play—it was to see a guy named Gove Scrivner perform. He absolutely floored me. He was playing with a bass player named Harry Daily, who would later go on to play with Jimmy Buffett. The two of them together were fantastic. What really struck me about Gove wasn't just how well he played—it was how he pulled people in. He knew how to hold a room. He made the audience feel like they were part of the evening instead of just watching it. I studied that. I decided to pattern my stage presence after him. The only problem was he was miles ahead of me musically.

I started playing at the Red Mule and loved it. Most nights, it was pretty quiet. I didn't have a following, and I couldn't draw a crowd on my name alone. Usually, there were just a handful of people scattered around the room, nursing drinks and half-listening. Looking back, I suspect one of the reasons they kept booking me was because I had a pretty decent PA system. Gove had even used it once or twice. Then one night, everything changed.

Charlie Daniels was in town for a concert and wanted to do a surprise set at the Red Mule. It was a hush-hush kind of thing, but word got out anyway. The owner asked me to open for him. The club was packed. I was terrified. I had never played the Red Mule like that before. I was used to off nights, empty rooms, and polite applause. This was wall-to-wall people, buzzing with anticipation, waiting for someone who actually mattered. That night, my nerves were shot. My hands shook. My mind raced. I don't remember much about the set except trying not to rush and trying not to disappear. I just kept telling myself to get through the songs. Looking back now, I realize moments like that are gifts—even when they feel like punishment at the time. You don't get ready for opportunities like that. You survive them. And if you're lucky, you learn something on the way out.

That night at the Red Mule didn't make me famous. But it made things real. And that was enough to keep me going.

Chapter 7

*John Hammond (or the
Dumbest Phone Call I Ever
Made That Actually Worked)*

By this point, I had been playing everywhere that would let me plug in, set up a stool, and not actively remove me. I was writing constantly, chasing songs the way you chase waves—knowing most of them won't amount to much, but every now and then one might carry you somewhere.

I didn't think of myself as part of the music business. That phrase implied structure, order, and adults. I was just a guy with a guitar, a notebook, and an unreasonable amount of faith. I wanted to make some kind of progress in music, so I started doing what musicians do when they feel stuck—I read books about the music business, hoping the answers would somehow fall out between chapters.

One name kept popping up over and over again: John Hammond. I learned that if you traced the roots of a ridiculous amount of American music far enough back, you eventually ran into John Hammond standing there calmly, holding a clipboard, saying, "Yes. That one." He wasn't flashy. He wasn't a hitmaker in the modern sense. He didn't chase trends. He recognized truth. Early. Before it was safe. Before it was popular.

He had been responsible—directly or indirectly—for Billie Holiday, Count Basie, Bob Dylan, Bruce Springsteen, Aretha Franklin, and Stevie Ray Vaughan, just a few names. That's not a résumé. That's a diagnosis.

One day at the library, I picked up a *Who's Who* book, flipped through it, and there he was. Name. Address. Phone number. Perfect. I wrote the information down, went home, and decided this was the man who was going to help me with my music career. No hesitation. No doubt. I had cracked the system. I didn't know what I was supposed to say—"Hello, sir, I'm nobody, but I have some feelings and a guitar?" There was no version of this that sounded sane. Eventually, I did what I always did when I was terrified. I picked up the phone.

THE CALL

"Hello?"

I froze. Hello? That was him. The actual John Hammond. The guy who discovered Dylan. I wasn't ready for this.

"Uh ... hello. Mr. Hammond? My name is Tom Sykes. I'm a musician, and I need some help.

There was a pause.

"I'm on my way to the opera with my wife," he said. "Don't call me at home." Click.

I sat there stunned for a second...then did the only logical thing. I called back.

"Hello?""Mr. Hammond, I'm sorry to bother you again, but I don't have your office number." He rattled off the number and said, "How did you get my home phone number?" I told him it was listed in a *Who's Who* book. He muttered, "That's just great," and hung up again.

I sat there holding the phone, listening to that beeping sound it makes when you've officially pushed things too far. I wondered if I had just destroyed the biggest opportunity of my life in under sixty seconds.

I didn't sleep much that night. I kept replaying the call in my head, wondering if he would ever talk to me again—or if my name was now taped to his phone with the words DO NOT ANSWER written next to it. The next morning, I paced around like a nervous dog, waiting for his office to open. Around eleven, I finally worked up the courage to call.

He answered.

"Mr. Hammond, my name is Tom Sykes. I'm the one who called you last night."

"Look, son," he said, "I'm sorry if I was rude, but I don't allow just anyone to call me at home. What is it you want from me?"

I told him I was a guitarist and songwriter from Virginia, and that he needed to hear me.

There was a long pause. "Tom, you can't just call me out of the blue and expect me to drop everything. I'm extremely busy."

I apologized, thanked him for his time, and asked if he knew of anyone else who might help me.

Another pause. Finally, he said, "I tell you what. I want to meet you. Can you come to New York? Bring your guitar. How about next Wednesday morning?" I nearly passed out. We made arrangements, and when I hung up the phone, I was in complete hog heaven.

I spent the week typing lyrics, practicing nonstop, and convincing myself I was about to become the next big rock star. I flew to New York the night before because there was no way I was missing this meeting.

On the plane, I sat next to a farmer from the Eastern Shore who talked for twenty minutes straight about pumping gas into tomatoes. I stared out the window, imagining tomatoes floating through the sky like balloons, and wondered if this was a sign.

Newark Airport felt like stepping into another universe. Everyone was in a hurry. I was pretty sure if I stopped moving, I'd be trampled. I got in a cab, and before my ass hit the seat, the driver slammed the meter down, hit the gas, and started yelling at other cars.

"Where are you going?" he demanded. I started explaining I had a meeting with John Hammond. "I don't want your life story," he said. "Just tell me where the fuck to take you."

"The Abbey Victoria Hotel on Fifty-First."

"Now was that so fucking hard?" he said, immediately screaming "MORON" out the window at another driver. I lit a cigarette and prayed Joey from Jersey didn't end my career before it started. The city was overwhelming.

Who John Hammond actually was, before I go any further—it's important to understand why this mattered. John Hammond didn't discover people in the way talent shows pretend discovery works. He didn't manufacture artists. He didn't mold anyone into something else. He protected them. He believed American music—real American music—was worth fighting for. Blues. Folk. Jazz. Voices that didn't fit neatly anywhere. People who sang like themselves, not like what the market wanted that week. He had fought record companies over this his entire career. Lost arguments. Won a few. Never backed down.

If John Hammond wanted to hear your songs, it wasn't because he thought you were going to be famous. It was because he thought you might actually have something to say. That's a much heavier compliment.

MEETING JOHN

I walked from my hotel to his office at Columbus Circle, palms sweating, mouth dry. When he greeted me, all that disappeared. He was warm. Calm. Instantly likable.

"Why don't you tune up?" he said. "I have a few things to do."

When he came back, he sat in front of me with my freshly typed lyrics. I started playing one song and singing another. I was completely panicking. He read my lyrics at lightning speed. Pages floated to the floor.

"Stop," he said. "What's wrong with you?" I told him I was intimidated. He genuinely didn't understand why. We went to lunch. He talked about Dylan and Springsteen. He told me talent was rare and intimidation was useless.

"Go home," he said. "Make a tape. Get drunk if you have to. Immerse yourself in the songs. Forget about judgment." I left feeling like I had blown everything, but I went home, made the tape, and sent it to him.

Three weeks later, the phone rang. It was John.

"Tom, I want to work with you." Not Columbia Records. Not stardom. Work. He tore into my confidence. My hooks. My fear. And he was right. That's when I realized he wasn't interested in people who quit. So I buckled down.

WHAT DIDN'T HAPPEN

Nothing happened the way people imagine these stories ending. There was no instant deal. No dramatic signing. No phone call announcing that my life was about to change. And strangely, I wasn't disappointed. Because something far more important had already happened. Someone who understood the long spine of American music—someone who had helped shape it—had taken me seriously. Not my potential. Not my marketability. Me. That doesn't make you famous. But it does make it very hard to quit.

WHAT HE GAVE ME

That meeting didn't turn me into a professional musician overnight. It didn't solve my money problems. It didn't protect me from bad decisions. It didn't guarantee anything. What it gave me was permission. Not from him—from myself. If someone like John Hammond thought what I was doing was worth protecting, then I owed it to myself to keep doing it honestly. Even when it didn't work. Especially when it didn't work.

I went back to my life. The same rooms. The same drives. The same doubts. But something had shifted. I wasn't chasing a fantasy anymore. I was chasing the work.

And that's a very different thing.

Chapter 8

Bruce Springsteen, Witches, and Why You Always Call John First

John wanted me to go see Bruce Springsteen. That alone should tell you something. John Hammond didn't tell people to do things casually. He didn't say, "You might enjoy this," or, "Check this out if you have time." When John suggested something, it was because he thought there was something there you needed to understand. So I went to the Hampton Roads Coliseum.

They had blocked off half the building because Bruce hadn't sold enough tickets to fill it. Which, at the time, was apparently a problem. It wasn't for him. From the moment he walked onstage, it didn't matter how many seats were empty. The room belonged to him. This guy was great live. Not flashy. Not theatrical. He didn't work the crowd so much as inhabit it. Everything John had ever said about Bruce made sense within the first few minutes. John always told me that Bruce's records never quite captured what he did onstage. Now I understood why. Stage presence isn't something you practice in a mirror. You either have it or you don't. Bruce had it. He wasn't trying to be cool. He wasn't trying to impress anyone. He was just there, fully, and the room leaned in.

I became a fan almost immediately. What struck me most was that he seemed to be taking rock music somewhere else. Somewhere honest. It didn't feel like he cared much about fame. It felt like he cared about the songs, about saying something real, about connecting. That's always been the thing I value most. I've never liked musicians who spend hours on clothes and attitude but treat the music like an afterthought.

Watching Bruce, something opened up for me. I realized I didn't want to stay boxed into folk music. I loved it—but I didn't want fences around my sound. Bruce's band had this wall of sound that was huge without being hollow. It was emotional without being dramatic. Everything worked together. I couldn't wait to call John. When we talked, I tried to explain what I'd felt, which wasn't easy. How do you explain the moment something clicks? John already knew. He always did. We also talked about my lack of confidence—which had been tagging along with me like an unpaid roadie for years.

I told him I was still questioning whether what I was doing really mattered. Whether anyone would actually care. He would get mad and tell me that he wouldn't waste his time if I didn't have the talent.

That's when I came up with an idea. I told him I wanted to make a local album. Nothing fancy. Just record some of my songs and put them out there. If people liked it —if even a handful of people responded—maybe I'd finally believe there was something there. John thought it was a good idea. That mattered more than the idea itself. So that became the plan. For the first time in a long while, I wasn't just reacting to what came next. I was moving with intention.

PARIAH AND DROWNING WITCHES

I started putting the album together around the time my friend Alan Sawyer was moving his studio. He owned Commercial Audio and was relocating it from the back of his garage into a real building off Witchduck Road.

Witchduck Road has a history. Back in the early 1700s, the farmers had a bad year. Crops failed. Instead of blaming weather or luck, they blamed a woman named Grace Sherwood. On July 10, 1706, she was tried as a witch by ducking. The logic was simple: If you floated, you were a witch. If you sank, you weren't. Turns out she wasn't a witch. Which was good news—except she still died. The villagers decided afterward that maybe the crops failed for some other reason. Humans have always been excellent at learning the wrong lessons.

Alan needed help with carpentry. I saw an opportunity. I'd help him build the place in exchange for studio time. The plan was to cut a demo so I could raise money to record the full album. I didn't have a band, so we started scouting players—watching local groups, mentally casting musicians like it was a movie only I could see. I decided to write all new material. I wanted the album to be a clean slate. Alan suggested a band called Hot Cakes. I went to hear them. They felt right. I already had a drummer in mind and had been working with a keyboard player named Mark Arquette.

I loved the studio. Loved everything about it. How ideas slowly became sound. How songs turned into something you could actually feel. At the same time, I was intimidated. I always thought everyone else knew more than I did. Played better. Had more confidence. On the first day of recording, the bass player started telling a story about how he'd hooked up a toy train transformer   one lead on himself, the other on his girlfriend—and when they started sweating, it shocked them both.

And these were the people I was intimidated by.

My favorite moments were when no one else was around. I could experiment without explaining myself. Alan eventually trusted me enough to give me a key to the studio and leave me alone. Before long, I was recording other people too. That room became a refuge. A place where I didn't have to be certain. I could just listen. And slowly, something started to sound like me.

TRACKS (AND THE ACCIDENTAL AUDITION)

Once the album was finished, I had to figure out how to get it into the world. Making it was one thing. Letting other people hear it was something else entirely. There was a massive record store in Norfolk called Tracks. It was owned by Record Bar, and the regional manager worked out of there. If you wanted something to happen locally, this was the door. So I picked up the phone and asked for a meeting. I grabbed a few copies of the first pressing and headed over. They took me upstairs and put me in an assistant's office while I waited.

The assistant was making small talk. She was also very pretty. Naturally, I decided I needed to impress her. I asked if I could use the phone and dialed my number to demonstrate my brand-new answering machine from Montgomery Ward. It came with a beeper you played into the handset so it would play your messages back. I thought this made me extremely advanced.

Beep. Beep. Beep. The tape rewound. And then—my mother's voice. She was asking if I wanted a hot dog for lunch. I pressed the receiver tight against my ear, hoping she wouldn't hear, but the room was quiet and she was close. I heard her giggle. So much for my big business moment. She told me Paul could see me now. (I later married her. We have two kids. I think the beeper impressed her. Life is weird.)

I walked into Paul's office and sat down. Records were everywhere. I started telling him my story, and in the middle of it, he asked me to hand him the album. He put it on the turntable and listened to a few songs while I sat there trying not to crawl out of my skin. I've always hated sitting in front of someone while they listen to my music. I told him all I really wanted to know was whether anyone other than my mother and my brothers would buy it. He picked up the phone and dialed an extension.

"Hey Donna," he said. "I've got a guy here. You need to bring in thirty copies of his album. I'll send him over when we're done."

Then he asked how I planned on promoting it. I had no idea. He picked up the phone again and called the program director at the largest radio station in the area.

"Hey, I'm sending someone over," he said. "You need to talk to him. His name is Tom Sykes. He'll be there in an hour or two."

With that, he walked me over to the buyer's office. I sat there while she wrote up the order. I told her I'd bring the albums by the next day. Then I went to see the program director. This was the shortest meeting of my life. I walked in, asked for him, and he came out immediately. He asked why Paul had sent me over. It was clear he was just doing Paul a favor. I handed him a copy of the album. The first words out of his mouth were, "We don't play local music." And with that, he turned around, went through a door, and disappeared. I drove home disappointed—but not angry. I understood. That was the way things worked.

When I got home, my brand-new answering machine was blinking. It was the program director. He said he had listened to the album and they were going to start playing it on the radio. That was when I started to realize something important. Life isn't really about what you accumulate. It's about what you contribute. And for the first time, it felt like I had put something real into the world.

BEACH THEATER, EGOS, AND THE CALL I SHOULD'VE MADE FIRST

Not long after the album came out, my songs started getting a lot of radio airplay. I was hearing myself on the radio constantly. After about a week of that, I got a call—maybe from Cellar Door Productions, I'm not completely sure anymore—but they wanted to book me for two concerts at the Beach Theater. One show was opening for Robin Thompson, a local Virginia artist. The other was opening for Firefall. I said yes immediately. Then I realized I had a problem. I didn't have a band. So I did what you did back then—I put an ad in the paper and started looking for players. Somehow, we pulled something together in time.

The Beach Theater was an old theater in Virginia Beach, one of those places with balconies and ornate trim that had clearly been built in the 1920s. I remembered going there as a kid with my cousin to see PT-109, the movie about John F. Kennedy in the Navy.

Just being backstage in that building felt like stepping into a different life. I remember walking down long, dark hallways trying to find the stage. It felt like something out of *Spinal Tap*. I was terrified, so nervous that I started forgetting the words to my own songs. At one point, I had to send someone out to buy one of my albums so I could pull the sleeve out and read the lyrics. That's confidence for you.

The first concert went great. Robin's band was incredibly kind, and the sound engineers made sure everything sounded good. They worked with us instead of against us, which makes all the difference in the world. It was a real pleasure—one of those rare nights where everything feels like it's moving in the right direction.

The day of the Firefall show, the promoter called and said they were getting tons of phone calls from people asking about me. That felt surreal. Things were starting to get bigger than I knew how to handle. The second concert didn't go as well. The lead guy from Firefall got angry because we were getting a lot of attention. So angry, in fact, that he came out and had the sound engineers pull part of the PA system so we wouldn't sound very good. It was obvious.

After the show, his band and I went out to eat at The Jewish Mother. They were genuinely nice guys and apologized for his behavior. It helped—but the damage was already done. That night showed me how strange and petty things could get once egos entered the picture.

Everything started moving fast—too fast. I signed a management contract without talking to John first. I called him afterward to tell him how the concerts had gone. He asked how everything else was going, whether I was gaining confidence. I told him things were getting big and I didn't know what to do, so I signed with a manager. He was furious. He said, "This was about building confidence—not signing away your future. Send me the contract." A few days later, he called back. He told me he couldn't get me out of it. His advice was blunt: drop everything. Stop chasing momentum. Go back to writing. Build your confidence the right way. I wasn't ready anyway. He was right. What looked like a setback turned out to be a reset. And sometimes, that's exactly what you need.

Chapter 9

Atlanta (Learning How to Disappear Without Vanishing)

John suggested I get out of Virginia Beach and focus on my songwriting. He didn't give me a strategy or a five-year plan. He just said, "Disappear." Not vanish. Not quit. Just...step out of the noise long enough to hear yourself again. That sounded right to me. And conveniently, my girlfriend had just moved to Atlanta. So I packed up what little certainty I had and headed south, assuming wisdom and geography were somehow related. They aren't—but Atlanta still turned out to be the right place.

We landed in Buckhead, which sounded upscale enough to make me feel underqualified immediately, and I eventually found work at a small video store. Back then, two thousand titles was impressive. Every movie sat behind the counter in its original cardboard sleeve, like sacred objects you had to request permission to touch. It wasn't glamorous. But it paid just enough and demanded just little enough that my real work—songwriting—could keep happening quietly in the background. Jamie and I got married during that time. Which proves love is patient, kind, and occasionally willing to marry a man whose career trajectory involves rewinding tapes for a living.

What I really wanted was to write songs. I was never all that crazy about playing live. I loved the studio. I loved the idea of building a song from nothing. So I bought a reel-to-reel and started stacking sounds the way some people stack firewood. Slowly. Carefully. Listening back again and again. Trying to hear what was mine and what I'd accidentally borrowed from someone better. John had warned me about imitation. Not directly—but by example. He never chased trends. He listened for truth. That stayed with me.

ALPHARETTA (WHERE DISAPPEARING GETS COMPLICATED)

Eventually, I worked my way up to store manager, and they gave me a store in Alpharetta, Georgia—a suburb way north of Atlanta. And when I say north, I don't mean the North. Oh no. This was the edge of Klan country. People would ask where I was from. When I said Virginia, they'd squint.

"Oh. A Yankee."

"No," I'd say. "Virginia is a Southern state."

They'd shake their heads like I'd just insulted cornbread. Atlanta was strange that way. It was full of contradictions. Old ideas bumping into new ones. Tradition clashing with change. And somewhere in the middle of all that, I was quietly working on songs, trying to shape something honest out of tape, time, and repetition. I didn't know where it was all headed yet. But I knew I was doing the work. And for once, that felt like enough.

EMBASSY (ACCIDENTALLY JOINING THE BUSINESS)

That's when Embassy Pictures wandered into my life. There was a woman named Vicky who used to come into the video store. She told me she worked for Embassy Pictures in the home video division. I remember thinking, "Why would a movie company need someone in Atlanta?" So I asked her. She said, "We go into video stores like yours, talk about our videos, and take you out to lunch."

"What are you selling me?" I asked.

"Nothing," she said.

"Well, can I have a job?" was probably the first thing out of my mouth.

A few months later, she called. She told me I'd have to interview with her boss, Alan. The interview went well, but I was a nervous wreck.

Jamie and I had just gotten married, and she had recently told me she was pregnant. The idea of raising a child on a video store salary didn't seem impossible, but it felt like we were going to be stretching the budget right to the breaking point.

Then Alan called. He said they were screening a movie and wanted me to attend. He told me to bring my wife—he wanted to meet her. I was thrilled. This was my first company function with a movie studio. Embassy was owned by Norman Lear at the time, and Alan told me I was now officially "part of the family."

When we arrived at the screening, I introduced Alan to my wife. He immediately handed me an American Express credit application—with someone else's name already on it.

"I think you gave me the wrong application," I said.

"Oh no," he replied, pulled out a pen, scratched out the name, and said—right in front of my wife—"That was for the girl with the big boobs I wanted to hire, but she wouldn't take the job."

Well, that makes you feel important. I got hired because a pair of boobs declined.

I was very proud.

What I didn't realize at the time was that I was about to start traveling. My territory included Florida, North Carolina, Tennessee, and Kentucky. I had a counterpart who covered Alabama, South Carolina, and Georgia. Suddenly, I was officially part of the entertainment industry. I could learn distribution, marketing, and sales—the things I'd known absolutely nothing about when I released my album, "Pariah."

My first trip was to Miami. Alan met me at the airport so I didn't have to rent a car. The first stop wasn't a meeting —it was lunch with his father, who ran the WEA (Warner–Elektra–Atlantic) branch in Miami. I couldn't believe it. Here was a man in charge of releasing some of the biggest albums in the country in his territory. I sat there as he discussed the albums they were working on and how music was evolving. I wanted to know everything this man knew. We went to Joe's Stone Crab. I had never eaten like that in my life. They told me the waiters made around seventy-five thousand a year and got three months off. My little Virginia world was expanding at rocket speed. Moving to Atlanta turned out to be the best thing I could've done. I was becoming more well-rounded—traveling, meeting people, learning how entertainment actually worked. I stopped calling John Hammond during this time. I was busy. I was settling into a different life.

Alan told me my first assignment would be with him. He said he was "checking me out," and if I messed up, he'd fire me.

No pressure.

There was a video distributor in Atlanta called Home Entertainment. They had a warehouse where they'd invite video dealers from all over the region to come pick up movies during what they called open houses. Studios would set up booths and pitch their titles. We had a VHS release called *Baby Safe Home* at the time. Alan pointed to a stack of tapes and said, "If you can sell all of those, you'll be about the best salesman I've ever seen." So while he wasn't looking, I grabbed a few tapes and quietly dropped them into people's carts while they weren't paying attention. Before long, the entire stack was gone. Alan thought I was incredible. The strange thing was, I watched people check out—and not one of them put the tapes back. That's when I realized this might actually be a good business.

Next came my first national sales meeting in Los Angeles. I couldn't believe I was going to L.A.—a place I'd always dreamed about. It was my first long flight, and everything felt unreal. We stayed in a hotel in Century City, with our offices across the street. The first morning, I woke up at three a.m. I was still on East Coast time and so nervous I didn't know what to do with myself. We gathered in the lobby and walked over to the office for the meeting. That's where I met all my counterparts and immediately felt like the odd man out. Most of them had worked together for years. It was the holidays. My daughter had been born just days before I left. I remember sitting at the boardroom table, feeling very grown-up, looking down at my watch—and realizing there was baby spit-up on the face of it.

The first order of business was territory reports. Regional managers started talking about their BPI. I had no idea what a BPI was. I figured if I could just get a clue, maybe I could fake it. Thankfully, I was seated at the far end of the table, and by the time it got to me, I realized they were talking about what percentage of overall business each territory represented. I had thought my job was handing out posters and taking people to lunch. Turns out, it was more complicated. They told us about upcoming releases and how they wanted them positioned in the marketplace.

We went to a Christmas party at Norman Lear's—or maybe Andrew Blair's—house, I really don't remember, where we were each given a huge box of candy. I thought I'd bring it home and tell my wife I bought it for her in L.A. Unfortunately, someone had included a card inside: Thanks for a great year—Embassy Entertainment. When Jamie asked where I got the candy and I told her I bought it in L.A., she asked, "Did you put the card in too?" I learned two things that night:

1. It's hard to cheat the system.
2. Don't lie to your wife.

A few months earlier, I'd been managing a video store. Now I was flying around the country, sitting in Hollywood meetings. The video business was brand-new, and Embassy was a major player. Some of the big studios hadn't even entered the market yet.

Our biggest competitor was Vestron Video. I discovered that all of us studio reps—no matter the company—were basically doing the same thing. Traveling. Selling. Eating bad food in hotel bars. And oddly enough, people were generous. They shared tips on where to stay, where to eat, which retailers were worth the effort. I sold *This Is Spinal Tap*, *The Sure Thing*, the *Princess Bride*, *The Emerald Forest*, *The Cotton Club*, and plenty of others.

Alan, my boss, took a liking to me and decided to "help me out." One day, he called me into his office, told me how well I was doing, then reached under his desk and placed a pair of old, dusty shoes on top.

"Do you know what these are?" he asked. I thought maybe he wanted them polished.

"Old shoes?" I said.

"No," he replied.

"They're Gucci shoes. And they say you're successful. I want you to have them." What do you say to a boss who gives you his worn-out shoes and beams with pride? "Thanks." I wore them for about a week, put them in a closet, and never saw them again. I'm many things—but a Gucci shoe guy isn't one of them.

I made lifelong friends during that time. Bill Kruger became one of them. At national meetings, Bill and Fred Eggins would sit together and crack me up. They'd developed a system of responding to questions, depending on where we were in the recycle. It didn't matter what the movie was, and that's when I realized this chapter of my life wasn't just about movies or sales. It was about learning how the world actually worked. And somehow, I'd stumbled right into it.

FREDERICKSBURG (THE COMPASS REAPPEARS)

Things were going well at Embassy—until one day they weren't. Alan called me into his office and told me they were eliminating my position. Just like that. He said he'd spoken to someone at Ingram Entertainment, and that I could probably get a job with them if I wanted it. I took the job. The catch was we had to move to Fredericksburg, Virginia.

We rented an old stone farmhouse, and suddenly I was selling videos to video stores for a distributor instead of working for a studio. It felt like a step down. The difference between the two jobs became clear pretty quickly. At the studio, you talked about selling things. At a distribution company, you actually had to sell something. At the studio, no one could ever really prove whether anything sold or not. It was the perfect job for a musician. Distribution, on the other hand, was about numbers, accountability, and results.

The farmhouse, though—that part I loved. The house had a basement, which immediately became my studio. Thick stone walls. Quiet. Isolation. It was a great old house, and it felt like a place where you could disappear in a good way.

One day I walked out the front door and noticed a squirrel across the yard. When he saw me, he popped his head up and started loping toward me. I thought this was interesting—until he kept coming. I backed up. He kept coming. I ran inside and shut the screen door. The squirrel came right up to the door and stared in. I started wondering if he had rabies. Turns out the previous tenant had been feeding him. I went to the grocery store, bought some peanuts, and held them out. He came over and took them right out of my hand. After that, we had an understanding.

I started talking with John Hammond again, and he asked me to send him a tape of what I'd been working on. I was always working on something, trying to develop as an artist. The reel-to-reel tape recorder I had was not enough for what I wanted to send to John. That meant I needed a real studio. I started looking around and found one called Wally Cleavers. How do you not go to a studio named Wally Cleavers? The studio was run by Peter Bonta, a great musician and a genuinely kind person. He worked with a lot of artists from the Washington, D.C., area. When I first met him, he was just starting to do work with Mary Chapin Carpenter. I've always been insecure about my abilities and easily intimidated, but Peter had a way of putting me at ease. I loved working with him. He encouraged me to push harder—to go places musically I hadn't gone before. He challenged me without making me feel small, which is a rare thing. Those sessions mattered to me, even if none of them survived. They only exist in memory.

Before I really had a chance to settle into this new life, Embassy called again. They asked if I'd take a job as a regional manager, this time working out of Chicago. I didn't hesitate. I jumped at it. And just like that, Fredericksburg became another chapter—brief, strange, and quietly important before the story moved on again.

WHAT JOHN NEVER HAD TO SAY

Looking back, John never told me what to do. He just kept pointing—quietly—toward the work. Whenever I chased noise, things got weird. Whenever I slowed down and listened, something real happened. Atlanta didn't make me famous. Embassy didn't make me fulfilled. But disappearing —the right way—made me honest again. And that, as it turns out, was the whole point.

Chapter 10

Chicago, Nashville, Atlanta, Dallas (Or: Failing Up with Confidence)

Chicago came next. Embassy Home Entertainment had been sold to Coca-Cola, which immediately explained the confusion, the meetings, and the sudden urge to restructure everything that was already working. They carved out one of the labels they owned—Charter Entertainment—and somehow I landed there as a regional manager.

My parents threw us a going-away party. I think they were relieved. My cousins were convinced I was moving next door to Al Capone. Chicago, to them, was still a black-and-white movie populated entirely by gangsters chewing toothpicks and firing Tommy guns out of car windows. Most of them hadn't traveled much farther than Virginia or North Carolina, so Chicago might as well have been Mars.

What I learned almost immediately was that I had never, in my life, experienced cold. Chicago cold isn't weather—it's a personality trait. We moved in January, which remains one of the worst decisions I've ever made, right up there with stapling condoms to sales sheets. We landed in Downers Grove, a western suburb. The first night in the house, I heard clanging, banging, and two people screaming at each other outside our bedroom window. It sounded exactly like Fred and Wilma Flintstone having a domestic dispute. I lay there thinking, "Well, this is how it ends." Turns out they were very nice people.

I developed a theory that people in Chicago talk so loudly so they can hear each other through their earmuffs.

The house had a basement, which immediately became my studio. This was a recurring theme in my life. Give me a basement, a shed, a spare room, or a furnace closet, and I'd try to make music in it.

Charter gave me an office in Oak Brook, but when they closed it and told us to work from home, I was thrilled. I've always done my best thinking alone, preferably surrounded by questionable wiring.

Charter specialized in what were politely referred to as "B titles." And when I say B, I'm being generous. These were films that felt like they had been written, shot, and edited during a lunch break. My favorite was *Emanon*—which is "No Name" spelled backward, in case you were wondering how much thought went into it. They flew us to Palm Springs for a meeting and insisted we watch the film and come up with a marketing plan. I went to a drugstore, bought index cards and an enema bag, wrote EMANON—BEND OVER, THE MOVIE'S COMING, on a card, and taped it to the bag.

It killed with my coworkers.

My boss did not laugh.

We had a movie about call girls, and someone decided to send condoms to retailers as a promotion. Unfortunately, they stapled the condoms to the sales sheets through the center of the rubber. Our lawyer nearly passed out. The idea was scrapped—after someone had already ordered ten thousand rubbers. Those rubbers didn't disappear. They started showing up in our weekly sales pouches. You should've seen my wife's face when I opened one. "Why," she asked carefully, "is your office mailing you bags of condoms?" There are questions you cannot answer without sounding guilty.

It was in that basement—my studio, though technically also the furnace room—that I got a call from Mikey telling me John Hammond had died. I had just started writing again. We had our second child. I was finally settling into the job and trying to focus the way John had always encouraged me to—quietly, patiently, without chasing noise. The news hit hard. John had been a constant—never loud, never pushy. Just steady. He believed in artists long before it was fashionable, and he trusted instincts when the world demanded proof. I realized I hadn't done exactly what he'd asked. I hadn't disappeared long enough. I assumed he'd always be there. I had just bought a Casio keyboard with a built-in sequencer and planned to make a demo for him. That plan was gone.

Not long after, Embassy sold the home entertainment division again—this time to Nelson Holding Company out of British Columbia. Charter sales reps were folded back into Embassy, and suddenly we were all Nelson employees. We were working on *The Princess Bride* at the time. Everyone was nervous about layoffs. We were right. The last film I sold for them was *The Last Emperor*, which went on to win nine Academy Awards. It felt like an odd full circle—ending on something genuinely great. It was a good little company while it lasted. And like so many things in my life, it ended just as I was getting my footing again.

Nashville came next. Vestron Video offered me a job as a regional director based out of Nashville. Nelson was clearly on its last legs, so I took it. At the time, Vestron was the largest independent video distribution company in the

United States. It felt like a smart move. So we packed up
and moved from ...

CHICAGO TO NASHVILLE.

We rented a small house, and out back was a storage shed
that I immediately upgraded into an office/studio. We
called it the Little Office on the Prairie, mostly because it
had electricity but still felt legally questionable. At some
point, I put pink flamingos outside the door. No reason. No
explanation. It just felt right—like the shed needed a little
dignity, or at least witnesses. I couldn't have been happier. I
was finally in Music City. I had convinced Vestron to let me
work out of Nashville instead of Atlanta, and in my mind,
that meant this was the moment I was going to get serious
about music again. I even got a bonus from Vestron and
decided to invest it straight into my music career. I bought a
Fostex eight-track reel-to-reel and the mixing board that
went with it. Yamaha had just released a new reverb unit,
which I bought, along with an AKG 414 microphone. For
the first time, I had a setup that actually felt legitimate. I
traded movies for a PC from a company out of Des Moines
called Commtron. Back then, video distributors let you
trade product for other goods. Studios would send you extra
tapes specifically for that purpose. So suddenly, I had a
computer, my old PA speakers for monitoring, a keyboard, a
drum machine, and a way to record without paying studio
rates. That changed everything.

The way I write songs has always been simple: start
with me and a guitar and build from there. Sometimes a
drum pattern would spark an idea. From that point on, I
kept adding to my gear. I wasn't going to need a studio
anymore. I decided to put together a four-song demo and
shop it around town. I wasn't a country act, but country

music was certainly part of my DNA. I joined the Nashville Songwriters Association and went to a few meetings, but I never felt comfortable. I liked Nashville, and I believed I'd eventually find my place—but it seemed like every time I started focusing on music, my career would wobble. And I had a family to feed.

Meanwhile, Vestron had a massive hit with *Dirty Dancing* and somehow took that as proof that making movies must be easy. So they started hurling enormous piles of money at one bad film after another, like confidence alone could carry a plot. We'd fly up to Stamford for meetings and sit through screenings of the latest "sure thing." By about the third one, the video sales team quietly rebranded the theatrical division Flop-o, which felt both accurate and charitable. It was painful to watch. We'd sit there watching this unfold, thinking, "What are you doing? You're putting all of us out of work." Weekly conference calls usually kicked off with someone calmly explaining just how catastrophic the box office had been. Then, without missing a beat, they'd say, "Okay, now it's your job to make this movie a hit on video." And somehow—this is the part that still amazes me—we often did. We moved shocking numbers of tapes for movies that had no business being successful in any format.

Vestron really was a great company, and I probably would've stayed there forever if the theatrical division hadn't treated money like gasoline on a campfire. That uncomfortable feeling started creeping back in: *Oh shit, here we go again. Another good job, slowly circling the drain.*

Two possibilities surfaced: MGM or Turner. A former colleague from Embassy, Martin, had become a senior vice president at Turner and offered me a role as southern regional manager. Mike, who I'd worked with in Chicago, was the national sales manager and would be my boss.

Turner was just getting into home video, but their catalog was made-for-TV movies—usually death for video stores. Retailers hated anything that had already aired on television. Their logic was simple: people had already seen it for free. Why would they pay to rent it? Our job was convincing them that a TV airing was basically the equivalent of a theatrical run. We even built charts showing what a TV run translated to in box-office terms.

I don't remember exactly why Mike left Turner, but when the position opened up, I went for it—and got it. Now I was in management. We were in the middle of buying Hanna-Barbera, and I was part of the team sent to Los Angeles to tell people they no longer had jobs. I hated that. These were people who had spent years at the company, and now they were starting over.

At Turner, I started developing plans for a children's music label under the Turner Home Entertainment umbrella. I wanted Turner to move into music production and partner with a major distributor. I saw endless possibilities—especially tying music to the made-for-TV movies we were releasing. What I really wanted was to build something creative inside the corporate machine. I got the go-ahead. Then Martin—my boss—lost his job. His boss, Steve, asked me to move back to Atlanta to help run the division. He promised great things were coming. So, naturally, we packed up and moved again. The great thing that came was him hiring someone else to run the division. He told me he needed someone with a bigger profile than I had.

I realized at this point that all my ideas and the music label were going down the drain.

When he said who he'd hired, I told him—politely, but clearly—that it was going to cost him his job. I knew Stewart. I knew how aggressive he was. Sure enough, Stewart showed up and within a month tried to demote me and replace me with his own people. No surprise there. I'd seen the movie before and had already started looking for the exit. I've always hated big egos. I never wanted to orbit them. I prefer my disasters predictable and at a safe distance. Stewart gave me three options:

1. Keep my job, prove myself to him;
2. Take a demotion; or
3. Take a severance package.

I chose door number three. He seemed shocked. What he didn't know was that I had already accepted a job with Warner Music Group (WEA) out of Dallas. I just wanted to start over—again. Even then, he couldn't let it go. He called my new bosses to try to get them to reconsider. Luckily, they shut it down fast. When I found out, I was baffled. *I'm gone—why make waves?* I called Steve, his boss, and asked him to make it stop. And once again, I packed up my life. Music was still waiting. And so was the road.

DALLAS WAS DIFFERENT.

We moved to Dallas so I could work for WEA (Warner–Elektra–Atlantic)—and I loved it. Absolutely loved it. I'd come from Turner Broadcasting, which was a suit-wearing, buttoned-up place where I never quite fit in. The second I walked out of the office each day, the suit came off, and I went back to dressing like myself—basically shedding a corporate exoskeleton. I learned pretty quickly that if I showed up at distributor offices overdressed, they assumed I was just another pompous studio rep. But if I dressed casually, I was suddenly one of them. Same guy. Different clothes. Entirely different conversation—and their guard came down along with the neckties.

The studio rep world was a strange little clique, and breaking in wasn't easy. Newcomers arrived with puffed-up egos and absolute faith in whatever nonsense the home office fed them. They'd march into distributor meetings armed with pie charts and graphs, explaining—very seriously—why retailers should sell their movie. What none of them ever seemed to grasp was this: it all came down to whether the movie was any good. Here's how it actually worked. The distributor sent out a mailer. Retailers glanced at the box art and decided if they thought it would rent. End of story. If they were on the fence, the distributor sales rep usually pushed the title from the studio they liked best. So the trick wasn't charts. The trick was getting the sales reps to like you. Take them to dinner. Be human. Don't be a jerk. That was the job—and somehow, half the industry never figured it out.

I used to hear studio reps complain nonstop and think, "Are you kidding me? You travel for a living, stay in great hotels, eat at the best restaurants in the country, and talk about movies." This was the best job in the world, and somehow people were treating it like coal mining.

By then I was considered part of the "old guard," which mostly meant I'd been around long enough to know better. I'd gotten into the business early—technically the second wave. The first wave were old record guys who saw the opportunity coming a mile away and sprinted toward it.

I wanted to be at WEA because I wanted to learn record distribution. They'd been the number-one record distributor for years. And suddenly I was surrounded by people who had helped build the most successful record companies in the world. I couldn't believe it. This was exactly where I wanted to be. The branches at WEA operated like independent companies. Each had its own accounting, management, and personality. A branch manager at WEA was king of his own little kingdom. My branch manager was Paul, who was nearing retirement. I was hired by Randy, who was taking over his job. Randy was a great boss—smart, genuine, and welcoming. He made me feel like part of the team. I also reported to Gary at the home office. Gary worked with the studios and fed us information about upcoming releases.

Every Friday we had conference calls with the studios—Artisan (now Lionsgate), ABC Video, Rhino, Atlantic Records Video.

IT WAS A DREAM JOB.

I decided I wanted to record another album. I scoped out studios in Dallas and found some incredible ones. One had worked on Stevie Ray Vaughan's records, and because of my connection to John Hammond, that felt like fate. Then I got the quote. It was roughly the price of my house. So ... no. Instead, I discovered that Cakewalk—the software I'd used before—was adding audio recording. This was it. I sold all my Fostex gear and jumped into digital recording. Suddenly I wasn't just a songwriter—I was learning about hard-drive heat limits and system crashes. All I wanted to do was make music, not earn a degree in computer science. Still, the upside was huge. No tape. Unlimited takes. Burn my own CDs. At the time, each blank CD cost $25 and didn't always work, so you could burn through cash fast—but it was worth it. After months of research, I finally got the system running. I could only manage four to eight tracks, but I didn't care. The freedom mattered more than the track count.

I started writing again. The plan was simple: record as much as I could myself, then bring in musicians to finish it. I was certainly working in a place that could help me if my music was good enough. I placed an ad looking for a bass player. A couple answered—she was a singer, he played bass. I liked them immediately, and we started working together. They knew a drummer, who added his parts after everything else was recorded. The album got finished.

So did my job.

WEA eventually fell apart, and I moved on—again—this time to a software company called Purple Moon, funded by Paul Allen's Interval Research. The idea was to create software for girls, who had largely been ignored in tech. I became a regional manager handling major accounts like CompUSA and Circuit City. They gave me stock. Supposedly, I was going to get rich. The buyers—mostly women—loved the concept. Time magazine even did a feature on Purple Moon, and I suggested my accounts be mentioned. It worked. The orders came in. And then, like so many places before it, the company folded.

All I ever really wanted to do was play music. That was the plan. Simple, right? Apparently not. Somewhere along the way I started wondering if I'd accidentally signed up for the "restart your life every time things get good" subscription plan.

Every time I'd finally get some momentum going—boom—something would happen. Life would pull the emergency brake, scatter my plans across the highway, and I'd be back at square one wondering who hit the reset button this time.

And yet, no matter how good the job was, no matter how comfortable things got, music kept showing up like that persistent friend who won't leave your porch. Tap ... tap ... tap on the shoulder: "Hey ... you're not done yet.

I tried ignoring it. I really did. But music has the patience of a Southern grandmother and the memory of an elephant—it never let me forget who I was supposed to be.

Chapter 11

Los Angeles (Or: How I Finally Got What I Wanted and Immediately Hung Myself from It)

By this point, desperation had officially entered the chat. I had two kids, school bills coming like clockwork, and a résumé that looked like I personally caused the collapse of several entertainment companies. If there were a warning label for corporate instability, my name would've been on it in bold. A friend passed my name to a guy named Barry, who called and asked if I'd be interested in working for a small video company called PM. I told him I was interested, but I needed a couple of days to think about it. Translation: I had no idea what he was talking about and needed time to pretend I did. I hung up the phone and immediately tried to figure out who the hell PM was. My first thought was porno movies. That was not a direction I wanted my life—or my marriage—heading. About an hour later, Barry called back and said George wanted to fly me out to talk. They booked the cheapest flight known to mankind. George picked me up at the airport and drove me straight to the office. The senior VP was there, packing up his office because he was retiring, and suddenly this whole thing felt very real. Also terrifying. Taking this job meant leaving my family behind while I tried to resurrect a failing division. PM Entertainment was based in Sunland, California.

After a long talk, my wife and I decided I'd get a small apartment first and see if the place survived longer than my probation period. During the interview, my new boss said, "Well, you might as well give it a shot. You couldn't do worse than the people we've got."

That was the pep talk.

I settled on an apartment in Burbank and immediately started figuring out how I could squeeze a recording studio into what was basically the square footage of a generous walk-in closet. Calling it an apartment might've been a little ambitious—it was roughly the size of someone's bathroom.

My bed situation was two air mattresses stacked on top of each other, which sounds comfortable until you realize it's just a slow-motion countdown to sleeping on the floor. Every night was a surprise. Would I wake up rested, or would I wake up folded like a lawn chair?

I bought a fold-out table that served as my desk, recording studio, dining room, office, and probably emotional support system. It was a one-stop shop for everything except stability.

Honestly, I was always about five minutes away from sticking a fork in the bed, throwing the rest of my worldly possessions into the back of my car, and heading back to Dallas before the air leaked out of the mattress—which, to be fair, was a very real time limit.

I didn't actually think it was going to work. But if there was even the smallest chance it might lead me back to music, I was all in. Or at least ... as all in as you can be while living on inflatable furniture.

PM turned out to be one of the most educational places I ever worked—and one of the weirdest. The building used to be a Jordache jeans factory. They had sound stages, set-building warehouses, editing suites, even a recording studio. It was like a dream factory that had been lightly sedated. They made me senior VP and later president of the home video division. My secret plan was simple: prove myself in video, then convince them to let me build a music division. Distribute CDs. Score films. Tie music directly into production. If they trusted me, I could help turn the company around. The films weren't badly shot. That wasn't the problem. The problem was the scripts—stories that clearly needed adult supervision. They'd make movies for about a million dollars, hire young actors just starting out, and then add one recognizable name whose career was politely winding down. The kind of actor you say, "Oh wow, he's still alive." Then they'd pre-sell the films overseas before shooting a single frame. Efficient. Soulless. Familiar.

PM always felt like it was hanging on by its fingernails. The action films had great stunts, explosions, people flying through windows—then the story would wander off halfway through and never come back. That's where I learned my biggest lesson: keep costs down. Everything else was optional, including the plot. The owners didn't fully trust me—and honestly, I didn't blame them. I was the outsider. Every time I went to lunch, I half-expected to come back and find someone else sitting in my chair, already logged into my phone.

So I did the one thing I actually knew how to do: I told the truth. I'd grown up believing that telling the truth was always the right move—in every situation, no exceptions. Turns out, Hollywood has ... notes on that philosophy.

Every time I gave my honest opinion about a movie— what I thought worked, what didn't, where I realistically thought it would land in sales—people would look at me like I'd just insulted their childhood pet. Apparently, honesty was not the industry's favorite genre.

I finally called my friend Bill Kruger and told him what was happening. He listened for a minute and then said, "Just tell them whatever they want to hear. It's not going to matter anyway."

Now, this went against everything I thought I knew about life, morality, and probably several Sunday school lessons—but I tried it.

And you know what? He was right.

Somewhere between diplomacy, survival, and learning when to nod politely, things actually started working. Success showed up, which just proved that sometimes the difference between failure and success isn't changing who you are—it's learning when to keep the director's commentary to yourself.

I met with the editor of *Video Store Magazine*, and the very first thing she asked was, "So ... what does PM stand for?"

Without missing a beat, I said, "Plot Missing."

Her mouth literally fell open—like I'd just confessed to a crime instead of explaining a company acronym. She told me it was rare to hear someone speak that honestly about their own company. I told her if you can't admit where you're weak, you'll never get better—and besides, if nobody says it out loud, you just keep making movies where things explode beautifully for absolutely no apparent reason.

Then I immediately asked her not to print that part ... because I had just made the executive decision to start telling my bosses exactly what they wanted to hear, and I figured publicly announcing the truth-teller strategy might not help my newly discovered career-survival plan.

Turns out, honesty is great—but timing is everything.

The first movie we released did ... okay. Middle-of-the-road B-movie numbers. Which, for PM, was an improvement. I leaned hard into release timing. Retailers have cash cycles. Big A-titles suck up money. Two weeks later, they're flush again. January was gold. Not perfect science—but close enough. Barry bought a Western called *Outlaw Justice* with Willie Nelson, Kris Kristofferson, Waylon Jennings, and Travis Tritt. I knew that was the title to prove we could play with the grown-ups. Around this time, DVDs were starting to gain traction, and retailers didn't quite know what to do with them. So I ran a promotion: Buy two VHS titles, get a free DVD. It worked beautifully. For the first time ever, they made over one million dollars on a home video title—which immediately raised concerns that we might know what we were doing. That's when I started acquiring movies for the company, sometimes with Barry and sometimes on my own. Apparently, "Plot Missing" was finally finding its plot.

Somewhere in the middle of all this, I sat next to a guy on a plane and spent an hour talking nonstop about music. My dreams. My plans. My CD. Me. Me. Me. Eventually I asked what he did. He said, "I'm playing on B.B. King's next album." I briefly considered asking for my card and CD back.

He called me later and invited me to lunch. It felt suspiciously like a job interview—except the only real question seemed to be whether or not I was an asshole. Once I passed that test, he started introducing me to musicians all over L.A. And for the first time, my dream stopped feeling imaginary. Music kept circling back. Always music.

My dad and I never agreed about it. He wanted me to quit "plunking on that guitar" and find a "real job." I never knew what that meant. What made one job real and another imaginary? The paycheck? The misery? I asked him if he'd help me build a guitar from a Martin kit. He was a gifted woodworker. He said yes. He got obsessed. He noticed how many musicians played Martins. He took pride in every detail. When it was finished, the guitar sounded incredible. It's still my main guitar today. The neck wasn't perfect. I had a luthier reshape it later. I never told Dad. Some truths don't need sharing.

I started to try to work my way into the artist community and started playing around town. I did a lot of open mic nights with a friend Jenny Yates, who had written some hit songs for Garth Brooks.

Eventually, PM was bought by Harvey Entertainment. Then the money vanished—appropriately ghost-like. I moved on to Showtime.

Showtime hired me to help fix their failing home video division and gave me a year. We turned it around. We launched Sundance Home Video. I became vice president. Still, I was always scanning for a door back into music.

By this time, I had started meeting a lot of musicians in L.A., all at different levels of success—some were killing it, some were surviving on coffee and optimism, and some were somewhere in between, pretending they had it all figured out.

It didn't take long for me to realize that my age had quietly become part of the conversation, whether anyone said it out loud or not. The industry loves to pretend it's all about talent, but there's always an invisible clock ticking somewhere in the background.

So I knew I had to rethink my strategy. Not give up on music—that was never an option—but approach it from a different angle. If the front door wasn't opening, maybe it was time to walk around the building and see if there was a side entrance ... or at least a window I could crawl through without setting off the alarm.

I also knew that meeting all these people was going to matter eventually. Connections rarely make sense in the moment—they're like puzzle pieces you collect without seeing the picture on the box. I just wasn't sure yet how any of it was going to fit together ... but I had a feeling it would.

I worked at Showtime for a few years, long enough to see bosses come and go like seasonal weather patterns. Every time I'd finally figure out how things worked, the leadership would change, the rules would shift, and suddenly nobody was quite sure who was steering the ship anymore.

And sure enough, things started to get weird again—which, by that point, felt less like a surprise and more like a recurring theme in my career.

The day I knew everything was about to change again was one of those strange, almost surreal days where nothing looks different on the outside, but everything feels slightly off—like you're watching your own life from across the room and wondering who gave that guy your script. Nothing dramatic, nothing explosive—just that quiet realization that a chapter was ending whether you were ready for it or not.

The day started like any other day—no better, no worse. The alarm went off at six, and I lay there negotiating with myself about whether getting up was really necessary. While staring at the ceiling, I replayed the strange vibes from the office on Friday. Something felt off. I was starting to feel disconnected from my coworkers. When I walked by, conversations stopped. People scattered. Whispering ceased. It wasn't paranoia exactly ... but it was absolutely paranoia-adjacent. Then I remembered it was Monday, which meant I was responsible for bringing donuts to the weekly morning meeting. So I sprang into action, mostly out of guilt. I decided to grab breakfast from the drive-through on the way to the bakery—an error I had made at least twice a week for three solid years. I hated that drive-through. Every visit was the exact same experience. A voice in broken English came through a speaker mounted in the face of a clown and said, "Welcome, may I give you an order?"

"Yes," I said, "I'd like a bacon, egg, and cheese biscuit and a cup of coffee."

"Okay. Cheese biscuit and a Coke."

"No. Bacon, egg, and cheese biscuit. Coffee."

"Would you like a new Hungry Man breakfast?"

"No. Bacon. Egg. Cheese. Biscuit. Coffee."

"Okay. Cheese biscuit and a Coke. You have a coupon?"

This routine went on for five minutes, and I still drove away with the wrong order. As always. As I pulled out, I tried to convince myself that a bacon, egg, and cheese biscuit was somehow healthier than a donut. I turned on the radio to check the weather and mentally escape with a song or two—only to hear two guys and a woman enthusiastically discussing their sex lives. Why is it always two guys and a woman? And why do they always assume I want to hear about their sexual exploits at seven in the morning? What am I, ten? Just play a song. Or tell me if it's going to rain. Anything. I made it to the bakery, got out of the car, and headed for the door. I saw a woman approaching, so I held it open like a gentleman. She walked past me without eye contact, without a thank-you—nothing. And that's when I knew: this was going to be one of those days. Then she ordered the last donuts. All of them. Six dozen. Paid cash. And spent fifteen minutes digging through her purse to find the exact change.

Why do women insist on exact change, while I walk around with fifteen dollars in loose coins I will never use? So now I'm forced to buy muffins. I hate muffins. The word muffin doesn't sound edible. No self-respecting man wants to eat—or say—muffin this early in the morning. I ordered them anyway, asked for napkins, and left, feeling fully defeated. On the drive to work, I tried to figure out how to dunk a muffin in my coffee after my biscuit without looking like a complete dork.

My new boss had a master's degree from Harvard that he earned thirty-five years ago and still talked about like it happened last week. He was constantly explaining how smart he was and how the idiots at other companies just didn't get it. So the best use of a Harvard degree was ... this? Not to oversimplify my industry, but I always felt we were only one step ahead of the monkey grinder on the street. This wasn't brain surgery. It was entertainment. The only reason I got into this business was to avoid working for a living.

I finally pulled into the office and parked in what was known as VP Alley—Mercedes, Lexus, Mercedes, Mercedes ... and then my Honda Element. The car that looks like a UPS truck had a baby. My coworkers hated that I drove it. After all, we were in show business, and apparently success was supposed to be loud, shiny, and parked right out front where everyone could see it.

Once again, I didn't quite fit—and honestly, by then, I was starting to think that might actually be my superpower.

NEW LIGHT ENTERTAINMENT

The president of Universal Music Distribution and I went out to breakfast one morning. Somewhere between coffee refills, he asked, almost casually, if I was happy. I told him the truth. I said I'd always wanted to build a company that did both video and music—treated them as equal partners instead of distant cousins at Thanksgiving. To my amazement, he said, "I'm in. Put it together. We'll distribute you." That was it.

Within a few weeks, New Light Entertainment was born. For the first time in my life, I had exactly what I'd always wanted: a video and music company distributed by the largest music distributor in the world. It felt unreal—like someone had finally handed me the keys and said, "Don't screw it up."

My business card listed my title as Lighthouse Keeper. The logo was the Cape Hatteras lighthouse—a place I'd spent much of my youth, including one very ill-advised night hanging off the side by my feet after too many drinks. The fact that I survived that still feels symbolic.

The first film I signed was something I'd seen at a festival called *Dirt*. We renamed it *Dumber Than Dirt*, which felt honest and on-brand. I liked the filmmakers—they actually understood storytelling—and the film had a loose, offbeat feel that reminded me of early Coen Brothers work. It felt like the kind of project New Light should stand behind.

On the music side, I signed Texacali Horns and Johnny Lee Schell first. Then came country artist Buck Jones, blues singer Teresa James, and others—Gia Ciambotti, Mark Fossen, Harley Krishna, and Lisa O'Kane. My goal was simple: music for people over thirty-five, an audience the industry had mostly decided no longer existed.

I was also working on an album I had started writing while I was still at Showtime. I met Michael DeTemple, a guitarist who'd played with Rick Danko from The Band, through Darrell Leonard of Texacali Horns. Michael was talented and easy to like. While he was reshaping the neck on the Martin guitar my father had built for me, his wife lost her job. Wanting to help, I hired her at Showtime while I was still there. Everything was fine—until it wasn't. Michael eventually demanded fifty percent of my CD sales. He'd played guitar and mandolin beautifully, but I had written, arranged, and produced everything. I offered him thirty percent, which was far more than most artists ever saw from a label. That wasn't enough. So I shelved the album. It hurt, but I'd learned by then that sometimes walking away is the only way to keep moving forward.

I'd originally planned for Michael to record a traditional mountain music album tied to overlooks along the Blue Ridge Parkway. I'd even spoken with the Park Service about selling it in their gift shops. We got well into recording, but the project was never finished. Some of that music later ended up as bonus material on the DVD for *Open Range*. Not a total loss—but not the dream either.

My plan for New Light Entertainment was simple—at least on paper. I wanted to produce films and build a music division that created the scores for those films, tying everything together into one ecosystem. The movies would support the music, the music would support the movies, and everybody would pretend I knew exactly what I was doing.

I also planned to promote the artists through DVD special features—which, at the time, felt like a secret weapon. People actually watched those things back then, and I saw it as a way to introduce audiences to new music without it feeling like marketing.

I knew the generation I came from still loved music deeply, but we were being fed the same old songs on repeat, like someone had decided we stopped discovering new artists somewhere around 1987. I wanted to create a music label that followed in the footsteps of Motown—musicians working together for a common goal. Music that actually spoke to adults, to real life, to people who had stories behind them.

It wasn't that I wasn't interested in the youth market— that lane was already being handled beautifully by every major label with more money than I could imagine. I just knew I wasn't going to win that race, so instead of chasing trends, I decided to build something that felt honest.

With distribution humming, I decided it was time for New Light to step into production. I came up with an idea for a low-budget horror Western to go straight to video. Nothing prestigious—just something to get our feet wet. I called a director friend, we tossed ideas around, and he went off to write the script. All I had to do was raise the money to make this film. A few weeks later he called saying he'd found potential investors. We met at Jerry's Deli on Ventura Boulevard. Two guys showed up who seemed far more interested in me than the movie. They said they were definitely interested. An hour later I got another call asking to meet yet another investor from the same group —this time at the Beverly Hills Hilton. That's where they asked if they could invest in New Light Entertainment itself. I said no.

I'd worked my entire life for this chance. I wasn't interested in handing control to anyone else. A week later they called again. This time we met at Morton's Steakhouse in Burbank. They proposed a deal where I'd keep controlling shares. They would finance production of the movie and they would give me some working capital. New Light would distribute. It looked like a fast way to grow without giving up the wheel. So I said yes. That was my mistake.

People with money often assume money makes them smarter. They took the horror Western idea and turned it into the worst film I'd seen in years. They renamed it *Shilo Falls*, which—if you're wondering—does not inspire terror. They named the production company Radio London Films, which also failed to strike fear into anyone. As New Light got off the ground, I realized something familiar. Once again, I was hanging by my heels—hoping the light would be enough to keep us all from crashing.

Chapter 12

Back Home

New Light Entertainment finally gave me something I hadn't had in a long time: the chance to go home. After nine years of bouncing back and forth between Los Angeles and everywhere else, I moved back to Dallas. The travel had taken a toll on all of us. I was tired of airports, tired of hotels, tired of trying to live two lives at once. Being back in one place felt like breathing again. Once things settled, I did what I always seem to do when life slows down just enough—I went looking for music. I wanted to record an album that would be released through my distribution deal.

I called my friend Marlin Adams with the idea of putting a band together. Marlin had played bass on my album *Something to Say*, and I liked him as a musician, but more importantly, I liked him as a person. At the time, he was playing in a cover band, but the idea of doing something original interested him. The problem was simple: convincing the rest of the band. Marlin suggested we start by talking to the group he was already working with—a band called Sold Out. They were established, rehearsing regularly, and already had chemistry. When we met, it felt easy. No forced enthusiasm, no big promises—just musicians feeling each other out. We decided to give it a try. We rented a rehearsal space in Dallas and started working through new songs I'd been writing. There was no pressure, no expectations. Just plugging in, turning up, and seeing what happened. It felt familiar. It felt right. And for the first time in a long while, it felt like music wasn't something I had to chase—it was something I could finally stand still with and let come to me.

New Light was my second chance. My correction. My proof that everything I'd learned meant something. I signed filmmakers who understood storytelling. I signed musicians over thirty-five—an audience the industry had decided no longer existed. And then the investors arrived again. They smiled. They praised. They talked about scale. They told me how impressed they were with what the company was doing and how much potential they saw in it. They talked about investing more, making the company bigger, raising millions of dollars, scaling everything up to a level I had only imagined.

And then came the real question—wouldn't it be better for me to just be part of something much larger?

It sounded exciting, and honestly, a little flattering. But I had been around long enough to know that when someone starts talking about "making things bigger," what they're really talking about is changing things ... and not always in ways you expect. Something that was big you may not have as much control of.

Even against my better judgment, I decided to go for it. It sounded like an opportunity, and maybe part of me wanted to believe that bigger meant better.

Slowly—and I mean slowly enough that you don't notice it at first—they began taking over the company. It didn't happen all at once. It never does. First, they suggested

I take some time to focus on building the music side of things while they handled the film production and video distribution. On paper, it sounded reasonable. Strategic, even.

In reality, it was the beginning of the end.

Little by little, decisions started happening without me. The company shifted in ways I didn't recognize, and before long, I wasn't steering anymore—I was just along for the ride.

Eventually, they managed to take the company I had built, run it straight into the ground, and push me out of it entirely. The hardest part wasn't just losing it—it was watching something that had once felt personal get turned into something unrecognizable. The low-budget horror Western became unwatchable. My voice disappeared. My authority vanished. I had built the lighthouse. I no longer controlled the light. What hurt most wasn't losing the company. It was realizing how much time had already passed. Music gave my life meaning. Work gave my family stability. And chasing both at once meant I wasn't always where I should've been.

I told myself I was doing it for them—and part of that was true. But part of it was for me. That's the part you don't like admitting. I learned that ambition doesn't announce its cost up front. It sends invoices later—quietly, over time, addressed to the people you love most. Music saved me. But it also pulled me away. The lesson isn't that dreams are dangerous. It's that they're heavy. And if you don't set them down once in a while, someone else ends up carrying them for you.

OTTER CREEK MOTION PICTURES

When New Light fell apart, I took a job with one of the companies whose films I had once distributed. They liked to brag about not paying producers. They said it like it was a badge of honor. I should have walked out the first day, but I didn't. I needed the job. More than that, I needed something—anything—to keep me from sinking into a depression I'd known most of my life. I hated what had happened to me. I replayed every decision in my head, over and over, like maybe this time I'd spot the moment where it all went wrong. *How could I have been so stupid?*

While I was there, I hired my friend Gene Zimmerman. He had been the West Coast VP for Ingram before getting downsized, then landed as a senior VP at a financial company. He was smart, capable, and miserable—just like me. Eventually, we admitted the truth to each other: this place wasn't going anywhere. So we did what we always did when things fell apart. We started something new. We called it Otter Creek Motion Pictures. We opened our own distribution and went directly to retailers. The biggest problem was money. Or rather, the absence of it. DVD duplication nearly killed us before we got started. I found a manufacturing company in Dallas and made a deal based on trust and reputation alone. They believed we'd make it work and pay them. That belief mattered more than the contract.

One problem solved.

For a while, it worked. We were moving product. We were surviving. Then the industry collapsed beneath our feet. Blockbuster closed. Movie Gallery followed. Overnight, there was no place left for the kind of films we were distributing. It wasn't personal. It never is. Still, I found myself starting over—again. Around that time, Bill

Kruger and I wrote a script about John Wesley Hardin and tried to raise money to make it into a film. But fear doesn't invest in stories, and no one wanted to gamble while the industry was burning down. The project never left the page.

I took a job selling video cameras at a small store in Dallas. It was humbling in a way I wasn't prepared for. I had gone from boardrooms and distribution deals working with movie stars and musicians to explaining features of a camera to people who didn't care who I was or where I'd been. But pride doesn't feed a family. You do what you have to do.

My father had died a few years earlier. My mother was alone in Virginia. Going back felt inevitable, like gravity finally winning. I sold our house in Dallas, we packed up what was left, and moved east. Starting over had become a pattern. Virginia is where that pattern landed me.

Computers are just boxes filled with ones and zeros. Somewhere along the way, we started treating them like answers instead of tools. I know because I fell for it. I believed technology could compensate for discipline, for doubt, for the hard and lonely work of creating something meaningful. Everyone now has a recording studio on their desk, yet music hasn't made the huge leap it should have. The same is true for film and books. The tools are everywhere, but instead of using them, we search endlessly for the next shortcut. The next plug-in. The next piece of software that promises to take us to the next level. The next level never comes from a program. It comes from the work.

Film, music, and books all do the same thing: they tell stories. Story is the center of entertainment. Everyone loves a good story. The real question is whether you're willing to sit alone long enough to find one—and then tell it honestly. Chasing success made me miss things that mattered more.

While I was focused on careers and deals and survival, my family was living their lives alongside me. My real responsibility wasn't building a legacy—it was helping my children become good people. That took me longer than it should have to understand. Now I have another chance with my grandchildren. Time gives you that, sometimes. Not redemption exactly, but perspective.

Books love to tell you that persistence guarantees success. That if you just keep pushing, everything works out. Life doesn't follow that rule. Sometimes it hands you things you never planned for, and sometimes you realize that what you were chasing wasn't as important as you thought.

I wanted to make a living doing what I loved. That didn't happen the way I imagined. I still make music. I still care deeply about it. But it no longer defines me. If there's anything I've learned, it's this: you are not the work you do. Work keeps the lights on. The people who love you—those are the things that last. When everything else falls away, that's what remains.

But now I know where the center is.

Not the studio.

Not the deal.

Not the next big idea.

Family.

That's the light I watch now. And this time, I'm staying close enough to it to matter.

It's important to chase the thing you truly love—and not let doubt or lack of confidence stand in your way. The path rarely looks the way you imagined it would, but every step teaches you something you couldn't have learned any other way.

I've learned that the destination isn't always the point. Sometimes the lessons along the road shape you more deeply than the success you thought you were chasing in the first place.

And no matter where the road leads, I'll never stop chasing the goal of becoming a better songwriter. I've learned that songwriting is a lot like fishing—some days you bring in something great, and some days you sit there wondering why you even bought the bait.

These days, I record music, make documentaries, and genuinely love the process—even when it fights back. I love the rewrites, the retakes, the happy accidents, and even the moments when I spend two hours fixing something only to realize I had it right the first time.

Creating keeps me going. It keeps me curious. It keeps me excited about what's next. And at this stage of life, that's a gift. Well ... that, and a good hot dog.

So if you'd like to follow along, you're more than welcome. I can't promise perfection, but I can promise stories, songs, and the occasional behind-the-scenes moment where I pretend I know exactly what I'm doing.

About the Author

Tom Sykes is a songwriter, storyteller, and longtime entertainment executive whose career has crossed music, film, television, and independent production. Over the years, he has worked with major companies, launched his own ventures, and spent a lifetime navigating the victories, setbacks, absurd detours, and second acts that come with a creative life.

In *A Long Hard Road*, he brings that experience to the page with humor, honesty, and a sharp eye for the way dreams evolve over time. Sykes lives in Virginia, where he continues to write, record, and tell stories.

Through long hours of rehearsal and support from his dog, he has managed to pull together a one-man show known as "Cranky Old Man With One Song." He debuted it last July 4th and is excited to report people liked it so much that they set off fireworks a few miles from the porch where he performed it.

A Few Quotes from the Show

"I told him to keep down the noise but he just kept singing." **Bill Kruger**

"I called the police thinking someone was choking." **Gene Zimmerman**

"What is wrong with him?" **Stranger Walking By**

Follow Tom

- Tom's Webpage
- http://www.tomsykesmusic.com

You can find Toms music on all streaming sites, including Apple Music and Spotify

instagram.com/tsykesmusic

facebook.com/tsykesmusic

youtube.com/@Tom-Sykes-Music-Documentaries

linkedin.com/in/tom-sykes-754ba5

9 798234 046970